'A brave and exciting new forum for t

'*Reactions* is a good name for this anthology. represented employ a variety of styles but they all share a belief in the poem as a vehicle to celebrate the uniqueness of individual experience. The object is to capture experiences that are as far away from navel-gazing confessional poetry as is possible. The poems take us around the world . . . but an unusual angle or exotic material on its own doesn't guarantee a good poem. These poets know that what draws the reader into the poem is the validity of the writer's reaction and their ability to express it in a language that is economical and sensual. There is nothing dull or predictable about this anthology. The title works two ways: the poems reflect the reactions of the poets but they also provoke reactions from the reader.'

*Vicki Feaver*

' . . . the poems are as good (if not better) as anything printed in the *LRB* or *TLS* each week – professional and highly sophisticated . . . On every page conventions are quietly exploded. An air of stylish transgression characterises this surprising volume.'

*Hugo Williams*

'There is no such thing as stable weather in literature. The new gathers itself around centres of high pressure and shifts, like isobars, around the map. It has been clear for some time that the MA in Creative Writing at the University of East Anglia was a generative force in fiction, and now the same thing is happening in poetry. Alongside the university, the Norwich School of Art and Design is also producing poets who have come or are coming to notice in the world of publishing and prizes. Such developments are exciting. All this activity has drawn in writers from other parts of the country. *Reactions* is the result. Here is a substantial collection of extraordinarily accomplished and varied poems, constituting an anthology of genuine significance. It is the weather coming and it is far more than regional. This weather will affect all parts of the country.'

*George Szirtes*

*Reactions New Poetry*, edited by Esther Morgan

First published, 2000, by EAS Publishing for Pen&inc, University of East Anglia, Norwich, NR4 7TJ

A CIP record for this book is available from the British Library
ISBN: 1-902913-06-x

Production: Julia Bell
Design/Typesetting: Julian p Jackson
Copy editing: Emma Hargrave
Cover design: Bill Bigge
Cover image: Barbara Watts

*Reactions* is typeset in Hoefler Text

Printed by Biddles Ltd, Kings Lynn and Guildford

# Reactions

## New Poetry

## Edited by Esther Morgan

*At the University of East Anglia*

# Acknowledgements

Thanks to Julia Bell, Jon Cook, Professor Andrew Motion, Andrew Walker and Sara Wingate-Gray for enthusiasm and practical support; Bill Bigge and Julian p Jackson for design work; and Emma Hargrave for patience and sharp sight during the copy-editing process. Thank you to Dr Anna Garry for her invaluable advice. Finally, I'd like to thank all the contributors for the pleasure their work has brought me and the readers of this book.

We gratefully acknowledge the generous financial support of the Esmée Fairbairns Charitable Trust.

# Contents

# Contents

# Reactions

# Contents

Contents

# Foreword

There's a special pleasure in reading the work that poets produce at the beginning of their writing lives: whatever it might lack in polish and expertise, it invariably gains in freshness and energy. *Reactions* bears this out. It contains the work of over forty writers, all of whom are discovering themselves even as they find their first audiences. Several have been members of the Creative Writing MA course at the University of East Anglia, and the emphasis placed on diversity in that course is evident throughout their work. The range and reach of their colleagues from further afield is equally striking. The achievement of the book is to combine what is actual with what is imaginative; to turn individual and personal worlds into a universe we can all recognise. It is an impressive and exciting collection – at once a testament to the strength of contemporary writing, and a bright hope for the future.

Andrew Motion, Norwich 2000

# Introduction

Reactions happen when unstable elements come together to make something new. Reactions can be unpredictable and exciting. They generate energy. When I was asked to edit an anthology of new poetry by the University of East Anglia, I wanted to celebrate diversity, rather than impose a manifesto or ideology; to present a periodic table rather than a single element.

As a teacher of creative writing at the university, I'm used to reading and enjoying a huge variety of poetic styles and approaches. This experience has taught me that there's no single answer when it comes to writing poetry, that there are as many kinds of good poetry as there are good poets. This may seem self-evident, but in the faction-ridden world of contemporary poetry publishing it is something worth re-stating. Both in my teaching and in my work as an editor, I aim to respect the individual voice, while believing that no one has the right to the last word.

So *Reactions* is not defined by a single style or subject matter, although recurring qualities are apparent: an outward-looking attitude; an excitement about language combined with a sophisticated sense of its limits and ambiguities; a bravery and honesty in exploring sexual and familial relationships. These themes were not specified at the outset, but discovered in the selecting and editing of submissions. What the poems here do share is a sense of adventure, a willingness to experiment, and a commitment to the act of communication. This commitment is characteristic of writers who write not only for themselves, but also for a reader, who break their silence in order to risk connection.

*

*Reactions* is the first publication from Poetry Lab, an exciting new home for contemporary poetry, born out of the remarkable creative crucible of UEA. As a graduate of the Creative Writing MA and subsequently as a teacher in the department, I've seen at first hand the tremendous energy generated by young writers coming together to talk, share work, encourage and inspire one another. The university's reputation in the field of fiction is well established but in the past few years, spurred on by the arrival of Andrew Motion as Professor of Creative Writing, poetry has come to play a more significant role. Poems of pertinence and power are being written at both undergraduate and MA level. Poetry Lab draws on this well of fresh talent at the university for *Reactions* and the forthcoming series of two-author volumes, *Fusions*. However, the Lab is not defined by UEA, and welcomes writers without any connection to the university. We hope that our reputation for creative writing will provide a showcase for excellent new poetry, whatever its origins, at a national level.

Inclusiveness is combined with an emphasis on discovering and presenting the best new poets; of the forty-four featured here, some are previously unpublished, some have already begun to make a name for themselves and nine are Eric Gregory Award winners. While magazines and local and regional anthologies offer outlets for new writing, it can be hard for new talent to find a space at a national level. It's true the internet has created an explosion of all kinds of on-line writing, but I'm in sympathy with whoever it was who said that using the web is like going to the Niagara Falls for a cup of water. There is a place for informed selection which *Reactions* aims to fill.

Its focus on new talent (of whatever age) differentiates *Reactions* from some other anthologies which largely rely on established writers. *Reactions* is planned as an annual publication with an open submissions policy, a listening post for anyone interested in contemporary poetry.

So what can be heard in this first volume of *Reactions*? Voices that are international in flavour, taking us on journeys around the world, from a prison cell in Tehran to a winter's night in the Czech Republic, from the eucalyptus heat of Perth in Western

Australia to the dank fenlands of Lincolnshire. Joanne Limburg's 'The Making of an English Poem' satirising the notion of pure-bred Englishness in both racial and literary terms, is characteristic of these writers' refusal to be constrained by national boundaries and traditions. There are voices that explore the hazardous geographies of the heart and mind. Read together the wonderful poems on fathers by Paul Batchelor, Polly Clark, Kona Macphee, John McCullough and Neil Martin to get an idea of the diversity of tone in the anthology. Other voices struggle with the inadequacy of language in translating experience; sometimes in the face of a literal language barrier, as in Julia Lee's poem 'You Mean You Don't Have Autumn in Vietnam?', Helen Oswald's 'Second Language', or Kate North's witty take on linguistic exile 'So You're Welsh Are You?', sometimes when a shared language is a measure of the emotional gap between two people, as in Helen Ivory's 'Just Words' or Matthew Hollis's touching poem 'Passing Place'.

My strongest impression is of the sheer wealth of subject matter. In this, *Reactions* reflects my own belief that good poetry can be inspired by anything, the everyday event, and the life-changing moment. *Reactions* moves through human experience from the spiritual to the mundane, from Hildegard of Bingen to PVC trousers. This is a restless book in which different voices engage with the cultures around them – I hope these poems trigger just as strong reactions in you, the reader.

Esther Morgan, Norwich 2000

# Paul Batchelor

---

## Brave Men Run

Brave men run
    into difficulties after the war.

Brave men run
    into old friends & keep their eyes on the floor.

Brave men run
    out of things to tell the wife.

Brave men run
    through your kitchen, your mind, your life.

Brave men run
    up huge phone bills: it's good to talk.

Brave men run
    before they can walk.

Brave men run
    into one another in History.

Brave men run
    because it lends a dynamic to their mystery.

Brave men run
    around to get things done.

Brave men run
    you into the ground to get things done.

Brave men run.
    if you don't you're an anomaly.

Brave men run
    in my family.

## The Vampire

> *Tom Collier hath sold his coals,*
> *And made his market today,*
> *And now he danceth with the Devil,*
> *For like will to like alway.*
>     – Ulpian Fulwell, 1568

The nights close in fast
& cold up there in the north.
Hesitation mists the glass before your face.
Few locals will venture out from their homes.

Our mam, however, watches the clock nervously,
sticks a tape in for *Coronation Street*,
& draws the curtains on the shadows outside
as they quicken to a frown around the house.

It always seemed the last possible second,
the final gasp of dusk before
night fully tightened its grip,
when she'd usher her little brood out into it:

me & my brother, like unwilling chickens,
clucking & fussing, knocking over the empty
milk bottles we hadn't seen in the dark –
then we'd all pile into the car.

Now we're off, over the lost, endless roads
pitted with pot-holes & gut-lurching dips.
Cat's-eyes startle up at us as we pass,
scattering hares, watching for bats following us . . .

There were many occasions when it did not snow;
many times thunder & lightning failed to show:
but I don't remember those times.
With barely a farmhouse for miles around

we bounced along the road's broken spine
singing *Cushie Butterfield*, or *Sir Patrick Spens*,
or asking our mam to tell us again
how the road was sinking because it was built

on the mines where Grandad had been buried alive
countless times, earning him his nickname, 'Lucky':
*One time A wiz doon – flat on me back –*
*trapped 'neath thi mud n' thi coal –*

*'n the blokes what wiz spoze t'be lookin forriz, stood*
*on me chist, so's A cannit so much as cry Help!*
*till the' start lookin' somewhere else . . .*
At last the road ended, with another mine.

Mam switches off the engine, and the anticipation
licks its fangs.
Darkness settles on the still car
like a suffocating picnic blanket.

Above us in the purple sky
a full moon poaches itself in the clouds.
My brother & I press our faces to the glass,
squeak crosses in the misted-up bits, and wait.

A wire fence and a floodlit watch-tower
mark the only gate to the mining site.

In the front, Mam gets over to the other side.
Adjusts the mirror. Winds the seat with a sheet.

\*

At last, we see him coming: a shambling bear of a man,
something in a sack slung over his back,
an angry Woodbine glowing in his cold mouth.
Thumping up to the car he'd come, wrench

open the boot & dump his stuff in it.
The car rocked about like a boat in a storm
when he climbed in, all shoulders and hands,
bringing with him a gust of sudden cold air

that chilled the car all over again
& that blue mist of cigarette smoke
which I had not then learned to detest.
His clothes would be heavy with the odour of the mine:

old earth newly turned: a smell that sticks
with you like a lesson you wish you'd never learned.
His donkey jacket danced with coal-dust as he coughed
or laughed (one fired the other) his underground existence off.

He'd kiss Mam on the cheek & leave a smudge,
and after a few seconds of unspoken exchange,
turn to us two in the back, & bellow
'HALLOW, LADS, ARE YIZ AHL-RIGHT?'

My brother & I would nod our pumpkin heads
and grin our pumpkin grins.
When this pleased him, he'd reach behind his seat
and grab at our knees, his hand swinging like a shovel.

## Rats

Hypnotic as the draw and
spill of waves across a beach,

hungry as the suck of the current underneath,
spat out across this embankment rubbish –

twisted description of a bicycle,
bloated corpse of a mattress,
bottles & tyres & chains –

rats leap
like salmon looking for home.

A sound sharpens the air
and pushes through your ear
like a diamond cutting glass, thrilling down
through the nerves in your teeth, about to break
into a birth cry.

Into a battle cry
as they order the panic that
creation wired in their spines,
keeping them charged & convulsing
like a sack of mangled threats flung open.

Each moment is Now.

Memories dissolve into instinct, & instinct,
like the tide that must test each rockpool, each cave,

carries on
turning everything over.

# Communication

### I

This stone is as stonily stone as any stone.

Once it was lava. It doesn't remember this.
One day it will be sand. And it accepts this.
Eventually it might turn into glass
but this is just a rumour.

What it must be to be a stone!
To lie on the ground stonily
waiting for someone to pick you up
& make you into a wall or something . . .

All the same, just a stone.

### 2

He sits in a café
flicking bits of flapjack off his notebook.

He has to tell her – but he hasn't met her yet.
He has to tell her – but he has nothing to tell her.
He has to tell her – but he doesn't even speak her language.

He could learn it, but he'd never
find the right words.
The right words haven't been invented.

All the same, he has to tell her.

# Lawrence Bradby

## Some Plausible Reasons for Splitting Up

'You've changed,' she said.
So I lowered my book
and calmly pointed out
that even as it bobs in the amniotic sea
where lightning first spannered together
idle proteins for a cause called Life,
Love is peering as oily waves lift it,
imagining landfall, proto-limbs,
labouring up the untrodden strand
onto a landmass new-touched by green,
in search of oases and locusts
and courtship and other things
yet to evolve.

She said, 'We used to be so close
but you've let a gulf open up.'
Her tone didn't rile me. I hit back,
explaining that when the jigsaw of continental plates was
                                                                    shuffled
just so, and all curves and edges
had puckered together like lips
Love was locked into Pangaea,
a perfect fit with everything else;
but hardened by earlier cycles of meeting, parting,
faulting, rifts, it couldn't stay comfortable,
worked itself free
from the Triassic heat and the dust

to inch round the globe again,
matching its curved margins against other continents,
chafing, colliding, making mountains.

'Yesterday our love made the earth tremble,' she said.
'It was bigger than anything. Now you say all that's gone.'
Up till then I'd given ground, made allowances.
I said, 'OK. This isn't something new.
There's scientific precedents you know.'
And as I was searching for simple descriptions of dinosaur
                                        wipe-out,

sudden extinction, the force of the moment
a mile-wide meteorite met the earth,
she was up and off, this time for good,
closing the door with an almighty bang.


## Standing Up for the Right to Lie Down

It was planned as a heist, as a scam,
our main aim the blatant embracing of peace
in public buildings and corporation grounds.
And what's more, to consume that tranquillity on site:
relaxing amid run-of-the-mill crowds and lazy attendants.

Cat-nap burglars, sleep-stealers,
forty-wink lifters, we planned to go in
and simply by sidling up to a bench in a corner,
stretching out, closing eyes, dozing
unconscious we'd regain what's naturally ours.

At Durham Cathedral, our first hit, I'd settled beside some
                                        robber prince
ensconced in pomp, and made a double bed
of his raised tomb, and thanks to my camouflage keks
spent a good half-hour cloistered in sleep,
before the bishop's censer clanked me awake.

Then there was Sally's Chesterfield snoozing
in the Member's Only room, Royal Winchester Golf Club;
and Dexter's much-applauded stage-nap
at the first night of Opera North's new *Sleeping Beauty*.

In these, the first few forays
of what became The League Of Stolen Zeds, our plans
ran as smoothly as Night Nurse from the cap.
Between the three of us we'd notched up,
bagged, an hour of publicly illicit sleep
without a hitch. The men at the front desk,
the porters, Security, they were no match.
We changed tack.

We let the press come licking at our heels,
carefully revealed the plans of our next strike,
daring the public to catch us napping.
Then in studios stuffy with audience and lights,
we took our places on soft settees
facing the steady soporific gaze
of Lorraine or Trisha or Richard and Judy.

## Cromer Pier

A bridge to nowhere
An airy street
A flimsy peninsula
A boat on legs
A knot of girders
A bleaching of planks
An Edwardian declaration
A coastal cul-de-sac
A balcony where far-eyed anglers dream
A skittle for floating rigs to knock down
A one-fingered gesture to the might of the sea
A toothpick in the teeth of the storm

A cargoless jetty
An altar to the chip
A stage for last-gasp entertainers
A static ship
A test for tourists with a fear of heights
Another reason to stroll the Prom
A floor full of cracks for the kids to peer through
Another surface for dogs to shit on
A majesty of poles and planks
A long grey arm with a lifeboat in its fist
A lance for the town to tilt at the sea
A trail of coloured lights in the mist
A platform so the well-fed fish can see us
A war medal pinned to the barrel-chested sea-walls
A trestle table on thin legs that take it high over the
                                                    low-tide sands
A coffin on the shoulders of rolling winter waves
A broken road to Shipden, Cromer's dead sea-twin


## Proof

He judged his exposition well,
that friend of a friend
who pointed out the minute light,
no bigger than a star.

We'd let our mutual silence hang like smoke.
Then, in the time it took to draw the last
from a longed-for fag and stroll back
through the french windows for dessert,
he tapped ash at the moving light,
asked, answered his own quick question:
'high-flying aircraft or satellite?'

'Watch as it shaves past a star,
that's the trick.

A plane blinks the starlight out,
a satellite doesn't.'

Indoors he hung some big ideas
on this small peg.
In candlelight his hands
sketched out for us the red shift,
eclipsing binaries, and more.

Not that I cared, off on plans
for the lucky meeting
you and I might have
that weekend.

Finally I contrived
an invitation
to your sister's second wedding bash
(same groom as the first time),

where I coaxed you away to the lawn.
Lying back in the dew
we picked out a moving light in the sky,
assured ourselves of one small truth.


## If Your Faith in Me Should Fail

just say these words
and from the concrete corners of the city
I'll call the plastic bags to leave their spiralling affairs
and glide this way
to cut a ghostly ballet in your street;

just say these words
and starting from the trailing ends
I'll roll up the criss-cross liquorice of the nation's roads
to a great sticky wheel at your garden gate;

just say these words
and pulling the drawstring that threads the sea-bed's edges
I'll tear them free from the land
to curl and reveal their black basalt undersides,
enfolding the oceans in a purse-lipped kitbag
that drips mud and drops shipwrecks into your lap;

just say these words
and we'll drive the earth from its measured ellipse
and take it where we like,
skidding across the sun's corona
to catch on the whiplash tip of a flare
and hurl back out past planets all with names;

just say these words
and watch the world explode,
leaving you floating in a clear white space
with just this piece of paper in your hand.

# Sue Butler

---

### Honeymoon

We catch a bus to Chernyakhovsk,
hitch-hike into Gdansk,

eat late in a restaurant, surrounded by locals,
hard drinking, patriotic, well meaning,
telling jokes so black
even you have to fake your laughter.

When the owner's sleeve rides up his arm
we see his tattooed number.

In our room overlooking the shipyard
the bed's mattress is stuffed with straw,
its pillow cases darned with blue wool.
Mice run furtively across our clothes.

Every hour until 4 a.m.
we hear the whistle of a goods train,

the men from the restaurant
summoned into the bitter night, to unload rivets
and aluminium, milled into sheets so thin,
when they flex the air cracks loudly.

To you it sounds like tanks in a street.
I am English, call it thunder.

## Tea at Claridges

Her slim hand emphasises the difference in rhythm
between Blok and Tsvetaeva
and when she listens to the man sitting opposite
it taps the table, makes and abandons
forays to the rim of the milk jug
from the handle of her white china cup.
Twice she almost unbalances
the silver spoon in the sugar bowl.

Halfway through quoting 'Kuk zhivyosta vam . . .'*
she honestly thinks she is reaching for cake,
ends up resting her hand on his forearm;
it feels like hide, the sleek muscles of a horse.
Instantly her palm is stuck –
for seconds, forever her skin fuses to his,
she forgets what she is saying,
repeats in a whisper 'Kuk . . . Kuk . . . zhivyosta vam . . .'

then she pulls, harder, a slight rip, then the tear,
even the waiter hears the tear.

* *From Tsvetaeva's 'An Attempt at Jealousy'*

## Glad

Smoke from a foundry chimney
veils the onion domes of the Church of Spilled Blood,
still boarded up but no longer used to store potatoes.

The swan she has been watching does not melt into the ice,
it flies away, a silhouette or a moment eclipsing
the golden angel above the Peter and Paul Fortress.

She follows it slowly towards Finland Station,
her bag lighter than when she arrived,
the wooden soles of her boots worn almost to nothing.

As she walks she hums Menotti, lyrical, *andante*.
In her pocket is a slice of Easter cake and a ticket,
hard class, one way.

## Waiting for the Rush

The door is shut to keep out sleet blowing in off the Volga,
she has to push with her shoulder to open it.

On a chest-high bar of polished oak is a row of china cups,
most have chipped rims, many are missing handles.

Newspapers lay neatly on a corner table,
she counts at least a month's worth, not one has been unfolded.

There is Siberian vodka and strong Polish beer,
a goose egg in a wire basket packed with barley straw.

The owner fought in Afghanistan, which is where he lost his
arm
He has no soup or cheese, so he boils her the egg.

She takes off her gloves, savours its warmth in her hands
but when she cracks it open something bloody

drops into her lap, its wings held out to meet the air,
feathers black, as if they have been burned.

# Polly Clark

## Dear Virginia Ironside

I thought my wife and I
enjoyed an excellent sex life,
but recently she informed me
that on the point of orgasm
she feels like smashing up the room
and stamping on the pieces,
she imagines breaking my teeth
and slashing the walls with broken glass,
she feels like a shark in a feeding frenzy,
as if she's drenched in blood
and no one knows her anymore.
It puts her off, she says.
We used to make love all the time,
but now she says she's afraid of something.
She lies awake all night.
Sometimes she even cries.
I want to comfort her.
I almost reach out.
But I'm afraid that if I do
something else will come out,
a deeper fury, even worse,
and I won't know who it belongs to.

## Road to Chisholm

Climbing the road to Chisholm, with
the mist weeping on the car, my grandmother
staring at a memory lost
in the verdant muddy verge, I saw
a galloping horse in the valley, orange
against the humbled green and the grey
mist-balls of sheep, galloping
calmly, like a film horse.
We climbed until I almost saw
the stillness of its back.
No one saw it but me. No one spoke, not liking
to interrupt the steady command of the wipers
or fight the protests of the rain drawn
beneath the tyres. In this silence I followed it.
Who turned it loose in such a huge place,
who left it in the rain,
who knew what I knew, that love had left us,
and this was all we had,
the rain, our bodies, a destination.

## The Passer-by

Today, though not in a hurry
(only remembering how it was
that my father seemed to break
the light around him, could not fit into it)

I passed a wolfish boy or man
cluttered in the street, splashed
aside by the rain of feet
around him on his slab of space.

*Spare any change* was what he said to me
in his dirtied words churned out,

not-really words, for not-really me
and though not in a hurry,

I didn't even murmur *sorry*,
I rained past him and over him,
or at least over his shape
battered dark like a rock.

Reader, I scrambled over him
like the horrified child of my father
who simply has to get somewhere,
somewhere abandonment cannot get to,

somewhere cruelty cannot reach.

## Metamorphosis

*It happens that I'm tired of being a man*
— Pablo Neruda, from *Walking Around*

It happens that in the morning
just before I wake, when the world
lays its palms gently upon my eyes,
it happens that my cheekbones are hollow,
and a damp pallor inhabits my skin.
The final ugliness of death,
like that of the sick predator
with slow blinking eyes, I feel it enter me.
Father, I've been writing to you.
I've been touching your picture.
I've been drafting and redrafting
your certainty that it wasn't over.
You wrote on a corner of paper
*don't panic*. Father, it happens
that your tired skin has been delivered to me.
Someone's gathered it up in the dawn air.

Someone's wrapping it round me.
My mouth's open in a death yawn,
my fingers are heavy,
my legs thin and untouchable.
I'm struggling to wake, but it seems so far away.
I feel a flutter of pain through fog,
I turn myself with difficulty.
Father, it happens that I die like this
each dawn, each half-sleep.
Later, when I am dressed, and for all the world
a woman, I catch sight of myself in the mirror.
Death has left a trace of its ugliness.
You've etched it into me, my heritage.
Father, it happens that I'm tired with the weight of it,
the knife of your face, the stones of your hands.

## Pilate Comes to my Father's Deathbed

On the third day
they summoned me, and I came to his bedside.
When I asked him, *so, you are the king?*
he merely smiled. I looked to his followers.
One said, *I do not care what he has done*
and the others said nothing.

It was a difficult case.
He did not express remorse, nor love.
His only word was *discomfort*
as the nurses turned him a last time.

I looked for a sign
that there was a case to answer. It seemed
that there was, and there was not.
I heard of no tenderness, nor compassion.
But there was a framed photo
and a daughter, and a son.

I said to them, *shall I stop this?*
and they merely wept.
I said to him, *do you understand my authority?*
*Speak. Justify yourself.*

He said nothing
and I was decided.
When the others could not bear
to see the drop of his head,
the sweating of his skin,
the blindness of his eyes,
I took my place by his face.

And when his gasps drew no air
and his frantic heart jumped
and his hand grew icy
I did nothing.
I could see no case to answer.
I turned him over to his own people.

# Sarah Corbett

## Wild Boar in Sarka

At four a.m. the streets were liberated
by the first snow. Half-cut, we tipped
from the bar on Staré-Mesto, stepped
into a moony dream, a black city glistening.

We were walking home to the outskirts,
Sarka Valley, where the city unravelled
to a struggle of brown fields and farmhouses, tonight
a village under glass in a snowstorm.

The saints on Karluv Most wore hooded shawls
of sugared lace, dropped iced almonds
from frozen hands as we passed – Christmas
coming again in February, only this time truer.

At Sarka the mouth of the valley was lit
with frost forming on the silvered drifts
and we remembered the boar that stopped a girl
last week, stamped, snorted, shot flames

at her crotch, scattered to the dark wood
where we now stood on the steep path,
snared by the crisp patter of cloven prints,
the breathy bulk steaming in the crystal night.

## Windfalls

Your neighbour offered his fallen apples,
the orchard thick with them after a sudden frost.
We filled plastic bags with the firm, rosy bulbs,
left a squelching nest of bruises around each tree.

We ate fistfuls all day, their sweet cold juice
on our lips and fingers; baked a bowlful
stuffed with raisins and cinnamon sugar
for supper, drenched in cream the steamy flesh.

In the morning you woke me, naked and alert.
I had to join you, undressing at the pump
in the ice-hard yard, shouting out to trees and river
the imperative of water chilled underground.

At breakfast your neighbour came. Laughing,
he had seen us, aeroplaning like his two boys,
ecstatic in our skins. *Jblka,** he mouthed, and together we cut
segments of fruit, the sap of apple rising from the knife.

* *Apple*

# Spook

I mistake a cow for a woman,
a sack of darkness, a black jacket
broad shouldering the horizon,
and I think – there she waits
for me to answer her slow coming.

She has been gathering flesh for weeks,
rising out of the dip in the field
each time I look, her white face
close, filling the window
with her wide-drawn eyes;

and here, where hazel have grown
to maturity in a group, a coven
even, a whispering hive, I'm sure
she balanced her handful of lights
on the wind between the leaves.

# Rachel Crookes

## He Dreams of Snow in the Month Before Christmas

Each night, the pad of feet
on the walk up to bed is as good as
a fresh fall of snow. The threads stretch
like a carpet that's new for each step.

The chill of it can't be caught, like breath
flooding lungs, the drip of a morning thaw.
He dreams of the snow that could cover him
when he's sinking into the bedclothes, a pocket
he split like a secret to get into. His eyelids close
like snow over street lamps,
the fold quietening the amber.

He dreams of the things that fall in the night, rattling
around in the bed with a convincing dream, catching.
He dreams of snow in the month before Christmas.
Not the dullness of waking, a headache
when the frost's gone, the drive caught under
a smother of dew. The dumbness of the early hours
as the horizon is muted by white.

## Keeping Quiet

We took a taxi back to his house,
lust like a passenger beside us. He sneaked me
inside, upstairs, past his sleeping parents.

The table was ready, set for Sunday lunch, shopping lists on the
side.

He didn't tell me that I wasn't welcome,
that his mother thought her son was sleeping
alone, kept at the edges, tucked up
with parents, friends not lovers.

He didn't tell me when he poured the invite
of a first night together into my ear.
He didn't tell me till I guessed.
Then he told me to keep my sounds down,
to bottle what gasps he made of me.

He kept as calm as the clean sheets,
as we wrestled and made no mess
around the bed, sex too tidy to be an accident.
While he slept I was awake, eyeing the door
in its frame, the desk chair nudged under the handle
so no one could find us sleeping.

In the morning he smuggled me down the hallway,
a dressing gown of his brother's my disguise.
He haunted corners to keep me from
the Sunday roast, broiling as we bathed.
He didn't tell his mother there were two of us
crammed into the suds of the bath-tub.
And when I made waves of the water and it crashed
to the bathroom floor, he muddled towels
over the flood, telling his mother it was just him,
alone and mindless. Not the clumsy splash of his lover.

He told his father he was going to get a paper
from the shop around the corner when he rallied me out,
clothes spilling from a carrier bag.
There was the rush of his goodbye kiss
at the bus stop, his father watching from the doorway
as his son ushered his unwelcome girl along.

# David Evans

## Just Talk

An American store might fit out
advertising hoardings
with neon, the English one, I doubt.

The equivalent is a board rewarding
those in recto with the word *tick*,
and those verso with *tock*, according

to where they stand. The trick is,
the board spins in the wind,
blurring the division like a flicker book.

Another stand might say *Fish – Chips*, the tin
sign blown so hard it needs a concrete plinth
to hold it down. The thing of it is

they never make a sound. The millionth
turn is silent, as is the billionth.

## Deny Me

You are me in your mountain climbing,
your bluebird over the mountain,
and in your incessant chiding

of, deny me, I will not.
You are me of black days,
of shutting out all but your black dog,

all but those black and white films I love,
*Celine Et Julie Vont En Bateau.*

I am the company you keep; it's amazing
the persistence I show.
You are all that happens that I note

in the flight log. A plane crashes
over Tical, and every passenger is lost.
Cuddle up, honey. Cuddle up, little dove.


## Desire

I want desire bordered by modesty.
To follow this wish I see
a thrush flying through corridors, its wings
not touching the walls. And from this thought leads:
*we like an emancipation which*
*can be wrapped into a blanket and put*
*beneath a bench*. A white stork in the soot
of a chimney. Riding my bike I switch
gears and begin to pedal downhill fast,
I sing, *my love's bigger than a Cadillac!*
and watch seagulls plague a tractor sowing seeds.
Witches' clothes
are strung across the spindliest black
branches of a fig tree.

## Cowrie

There she is, my mother,
collecting shells at the beach.
Her prize is the cowrie.
Cowrie complexity, cowrie complexity;
I can't remember which.

Not just one, but thousands,
until they fill a dish.
Then she takes their picture.

That is the shell of love, that is love's shell.

There she lives. Once it was just two weeks.
Spam; Rise and Shine; boiled eggs.

I bite on something hard.
What do you think it is?
A cowrie shell I've crushed between my teeth.

# Ivy Garlitz

## GI Joe in the Hands of my Brother

was shot by rubber bands,
was kicked off the bed's cliff,
was tied to our peke's neck
to patrol, cowboy style,
was run over by trains,
was buried to his neck
and left in the sunshine
until his head melted,
was mummified in tape,
lashed to a model raft
and pushed down the canal,
and was caught and blown up
by swiped firecrackers,
while my uncle gagged down
undiluted syrup
so he could develop
hyperglycaemia,
fail his army physical,
and stay out of Vietnam.

## We Sat Shiva for Elvis

We tore our clothes when we heard he died,
Mother and I sat on boxes
the full seven days. We ate boiled eggs.
None of the neighbours came.
They were glad we couldn't play his records for a year.
I kept my dates, got through all the songs, but I shook

when I had to look in the mirror
to shape my sideburns or adjust my shades.
I went to the synagogue,
I wore the tallis like my scarves,
but the Rabbi said it wasn't necessary;
when I stood as the only mourner

he tried to skip the Kaddish.
Still, on Yom Kippur I go and stand
for the prayer for God to remember
parents in heaven
and I ask God to look after him.
I think the King would like that.

## Love Is a UFO

You know you saw it
that night you were driving,
it was above you
hovering, then moving
in a way you never thought possible,
a figure of unearthly beauty
was beside you in your stopped car.
A light enveloped you,
but then it vanished,
leaving you in the driver's seat, shaking.
The experts state

it was a sudden flare up of Venus,
atmospheric disturbance, a common delusion.

You know it's out there,
waiting to encounter
the people who deserve it,
not the privileged few
hiding it away, or those liars
who say it's all faked,
those eyes that stunned you,
the bodies you remember from dreams.
You have to go on searching.
You have to disprove
that seemingly unshakeable fact
that you're alone in the universe
and always will be.

# Anna Garry

## Dissection

I used to like
those tall glass jars,
cork-stoppered, to trap
rats on their toes,
arms tangled mid-air
snouts nudging heads
broken whiskers
glazed eyes.

I used to like
taking one,
its formalin stench
the stiffened hide
feet twisted, scaly,
bright headed pins
impaling wrists, then legs
then tail, star-like.

I used to like
the scalpel
slitting from neck to navel
peeling back skin
slicing sinews
stripping the coiled intestine,
the grey lungs
a marbled heart.

I cannot remember when
I first touched bone.


## Lacrimatoio*

*If you collect my tears*, she said,
and handed me a glass bottle,
finger shaped, finely cut, a refracting stopper,
a phial surely,
for perfumes and oils.
*No*, she said, *Lacrimatoio*,
and with a push, I was outside,
my eyes prickling.

I'd be her joker, the stand-up comic
who made her laugh until she split with tears.
I'd hire videos, *Casablanca*,
*Brief Encounter*, *Titanic*,
anything to make a woman weep.
In desperation I'd leave her, then
sneak back at night for the sobs.

In bed I reach out for the place
she has never been,
meeting breast bone, a pale neck,
the hint of a chin,
stroking the path
where her tears would flow.

The next day it is sparkling,
making rainbows on the window-ledge,
an ornate test-tube,
beautiful and closed.

* *This is the Italian word for tear-bottle. Tear-bottles were found in Roman and Christian graves, and originally thought to hold either the tears of the dead, or of the mourners.*

## Strawberry

I was hunkered by you,
the two of us perfect.
You lifted the leaf,
moist, deep green, rough edged.
There it was, shiny,
a hundred eyes across the skin.
I was as you wanted,
surprised.

There was a colder day,
you were crouched,
forking weeds, beside you
whitened stalks piled,
roots splayed, like maggots
in rigor mortis.
I was on our step
trying the locked door.

The sound from my lips
I hear it plainly
like the call of a calf downwind.
You were only six feet away,
kneeling, your shoulders still bent,
heels lifted from your shoes
their worn leather backs
flattened.

## Flatpack

No one knew she came in boxes,
long, rectangular, two-inches deep.
She raised them up, a massive effort,
snapping staples, splitting cartons,
until after some manoevring
she glued herself upright,
all shiny doors, real oak,
the chipboard carefully hidden.

You could blow air through her.
You could open her up, but
there was nothing there,
not even the ghost of a coat hanger,
just white shelves,
in the corners
no dust.

# Helen Goddard

---

## Jam

Ladies, you know that
not being strong enough in the arm
to get the lids off newly purchased jars
of marmelade or lemon curd
or morello cherry jam?
Well, I discovered the secret of it one day –
that if you ease the blade-tip
of a dinner-knife into the tightness
of lid leeched onto ribbed glass rim
of jar and angle just so,
one deft lift gives out
a vacuum-ending pop
and the lid twists off the jar like butter.
You tell me why, then,
that sometimes
if there's a man handy
I'll pretend I haven't yet learned my trick
and will watch him force the thing?

## Babysitting Lucy

She said, 'Okay so do dogs
go to heaven too?' and I
couldn't answer. Look how
closed-up we grow, habit-
wrinkled, brains receding, grey

beneath the walnut skulls
(a wonder no one comes
to rattle us for freshness),
look how the questions stop,
how passion, curiosity shrink to
a pair of slippers and the TV guide.
When I said, frowning, 'I don't
know,' she clapped her hands in glee
and bounced, 'Yes of course they do,
of course they do, because dogs
love people.' 'Oh silly me,' I said,
thinking, 'Because of love –
heaven's because of love?' and
then something stirred inside, I saw
the cloudlessness of pure belief, felt
free, like in sunlight stepping off
the diving board into thin bright air
without once looking down but
knowing, trusting there is water underneath.

## Raining

The cat starts at something
that isn't there – what's she seeing?
It breaks me from a reverie, face blushing
from sitting this close to the fire.
Images of the Iron Man grown restless
are fading back into a huge figure
on a hill, then just the sky
over the hill, the strange landscape
where thunder is underground and jags
of lightning burst out of a thrashing sea
in an explosion of frost-edged grey
that sends cold through me. What does she see –
broken-winged kingfishers ripe for play –
or real food, already killed and served

each time she flexes a lazy claw?
Or is it the same dream, the man
who isn't a man, on the cliff top
with even the air afraid to go too near . . .
I go for coffee to the kitchen.
You sit inside wet windows at the table
with your back to me, eating,
your solid shoulders and the out-curve
of your back too big for itself.
I walk in as though catching you
at some sinister game, playing
with the broken kingfisher on your plate,
stabbing its coloured breast over and over,
grown restless while I was sleeping.


## Blind Together

They're making love – she's
thinking she's held down
by some costume-drama rake, all
breathless passion like a rage.
In her mind she arranges candles
just so around the scene,
adds a little rouge so he looks flushed,
checks her own expression but
her husband's not in 1999
either: he is nowhere, nothing,
swallowed, taken over.
Enclosed in a world made woman,
he fucks instead of weeping.

Sometimes he'll catch her
unawares and she floats too,
let's go into the blind space
that is all light, that is all
dark. Sometimes, yes, it hits
that they are blind together.

## The Rhythm of her Eating

She plucks the items from the fridge and swallows fast
like petals from a daisy in the yard – he loves me,
he loves me not. Uncertainty provides the rhythm
of her eating, it is a song without an end,
a novel she cannot finish reading; for each page
devoured, there is an anxious author filling in
the blanks beyond. It is a passion and a silence.

She is edified by food, it makes her real,
bulks her to the present instant. Blinds her with
stupidity. She takes it in again, again, again
as if attempting to brick up the mouth, the food
a dam against the words that want to spill;
the food is solid – each mouthful reassures
each mouthful reassures each mouthful

# Karen Goodwin

## The Year's Anatomy

January was skeletons, a clasp of bone
found by the iron blade of February

who called over the hill to March;
its sudden breath lifted the wings of birds.

April undid itself, unscrolled a hand
and May secreted hormones.

Musk stain and blossom made blood
for June, July's heart beating in a rose.

August, hot and dry as a kiln
itched for change until September

pushed its warmth from the door
like a cobweb. October was clear

with a mind for the planets,
chiselling perfection from the moon.

November wept for what could only ever
be shadow and December stone.

## To the Unnamed

Baby, I still bloom with birth milk,
it ripens my dress, two buds
where you should have been.

I am sweet with summer's juice,
a great bell moving
without a tongue to sing.

You slipped so easily to the hands
of another, small moon
nudged among the rock.

I wake to each day's distance,
your face melting back
to the river from where you came.

## Fallen Star

All that summer the roses
put out their thorns along our garden wall;
a bramble of wire that almost fizzled to touch it.

We were practising for gala gymnastics
on a rug of lawn, the grass flattening
under the weight of my body as I carried you
into the air on the arabesque of my feet.

As if the world paused in that moment,
the earth held sweet and damp under me,
a tangle of mowers digested in the distance,
your mouth torn open to the sky

before my leg buckled,
and the roses caught you with hooked claw –
a comet's tail of blood burning on your thigh.

# Eleanor Green

## Spaces Between

a fly traces his drunken course
on three-dimensional territory
forcing, only today, the realisation:
there are spaces between spaces
owned by no one – and awkward –
like silence on a phone line . . .

        Traffic – the middle of a junction –
        possessed by many, temporarily . . .

            Scent on breeze, soon lost,
          and travelling on, to be owned
                by another . . .

Who governs these spaces?
this single Lord of the Flies?
hovering . . . throbbing . . .
in his web of sudden highways;
in each square foot of sunlight;
for a moment possessing: nothing.

## Rehearsal

for an exercise
I look at his hands
to improve our relationship
onstage?
creased knuckles, already ageing,
wiry hair climbing his wrists.
can't help but imagine these fingers
resting, rough, upon bare flesh,
mine?
and the longer I observe, the more strange
are these veined creatures,
moving under my fingers' command
crowded with blood and power,
his?
relaxed, their heaviness overwhelms,
as if holding his entire body,
now dislocated,
but for that growing dampness,
inescapable when palms,
ours?
meet.

soon – how they might be in forty years
clouds my vision of them now,
and the time between lies sleeping
inside innocent plasma and tissue.

I looked at his hands until
they were hands no longer.

# Jane Griffiths

## Still Life

The hands. Like crêpe paper flowers
unfurling in water, their colours bleeding
down the ribbed skin, veins purple
to off-white and the links in the palm
growing tight as if life-lines were high-
wires, not lines of containment.

Monochrome, there's a card between
the flowers: the sun just setting,
or perhaps the moon just rising,
and against the moon, or sun,
a couple of posts, three wires
and a shadow like nothing so much

as an amputee spider, a starfish.
It's the old unicycle trick: no
hands and just his curling coat-
tails for balance (even these,
it seems, are tied behind his back).
How quickly he must be moving,

in defiance of the black and white
static, eyes fixed on the point of
vanishing as if there were no roofs
below, no hospitals, flowers or
spectators blinking fishily up
through the dull light, as if air were

buoyant as water, and to disappear
just a final step leaving no evidence
but these hands with their palmed
secrets, furled tightly shut as if in
fear their score might somehow
still be possible to follow.

## Fantasia

So go, if you're going. Why wait? Traffic is staccato
down the High: it throbs and strums. The clock
on the dashboard shows a quick green pulse. I fiddle
with the faulty tape-deck and think about electricity,

crossed wires, about your voice as it might sound
out there: all that wow and flutter echoic among
the stars and the lights on the switchboard
tracking your vocals as they stalk the world on stilts

like compasses promising the word itself and not
a dot dot dash encoding the vowels cradled (crystellar,
vibrato) in your voice-box, the transatlantically
bated breath and the long and the short of it –

*Hell*, you say. *Hell, we'll be late*. We're up to the hilt
in it; we're up to the traffic control. Two men swivel
boards: messages flick taut as patball. Stop. Go.
Concentrate. Don't look now: they are signing privately,

single-mindedly: one car, two lorries. One minute. Wait.
Palm fingers. And swivel. They are synchronized. Stop.
Go. Don't go. This could take some time. *Hell*,
you say again, stuttering through the undertow

of a kerbside drill. The street is a beatbox, the pulse
is continuous, the dashboard clock shows that, yes,

we're irremediably, irredeemably late and the waste
and the shame of it is, it's not that we weren't counting –

not as if we'd slipped from sight down the back-rests,
ignored the signs, palmed fingers, let the furious
claxophony wash over our heads; not as if we'd managed
even one throwaway line, laughing sidelong and seeing

all the tension unravel like a tape sprung from its cover
in lavish irridescent streamers embellishing bumpers,
wing-mirrors and exhaust pipes from Queen's down
to Carfax, and volatile as if the hooters were a send-off

and the traffic jam a procession, as if our approach saw
all the signals turn green for go while the tape went wild
with static and wowed and dropped out, running rings
round the whole twin-track of recorded history.

## Anecdotal

She said Oxford, for her, was a view
from the bus for Chipping Norton:
sherbet-dip and Opal Fruits,
and a nun with a canary.

A first-floor room on St Giles,
a blue chenille table-cloth
and several cups of tea. Walls
like plane trees descaling;

green tiles institutional down
the corridor, but as she went
out, the sound of singing,
and the canary pendulant

from a rosary. A hive.
A honeycomb. The skeleton
of a dinosaur, and the story
how, at Chaldon Herring

in the nineteenth century
the exiled Duchesse de Berri
and retinue found human
remains, throned and shouldering

antlers as a bird bears wings.
There was no shaking, she said,
the thought of them, furred
and gowned in the very rich

hours, in hats like foliage
descending while the barrow
magnified their murmured whys
and wherefores and the dark

swarmed like a honeycomb
around them and overhead
the grass was edgy as fret-wire,
the trees plumed like ostriches

and the moon shone crazed
and cagey as a halo, and all night
couchant in the barrow they counted
paces religiously and religiously caught

their breath, and never heard the song
at daybreak, but shuffled on,
and their front man advanced a caged
canary like a shaft of illumination.

## Orpheus on the Central Line

Much like any other busker
he gets on around Marble Arch:
blond, bearded, with a guitar
and an orange poncho that smells
as if he'd just come off the river.

His repertoire covers the Beatles
and *Scarborough Fair*; covertly,
he passes a small felt bag
for coins, but come Oxford Circus
he doesn't move on – instead

promises, 'A new song, one of mine.'
He wears dark glasses. Reflected,
the carriage wraps across his eyes
like a bandage as he tilts his head
back and sings not to, but through

the passengers, joltingly, like a faulty
electric light. A kind of lament,
full of vowel sound. Clearly,
he can't be seeing things right:
he sways to the music, and not

to the underground. But just
as people grow uneasy (thinking
they're stuck with a lunatic)
he recollects himself, and at Bank
marches off down the rust-stained

corridor, side-stepping the man
with the dog and the outstretched
hand. But he finds the spaces singing
with his own footsteps pacing on
ahead and the echoed warning to *Mind*

*the Gap*, and as he ascends the spiral
stair the light at the end of the tunnel
grows dimmer: each time, he winds up
turning back for something (he's forgotten
what) that he might have left behind.

## Paris, 1900

This must be a hoax, no matter
the sheer weight of time in its making:
whole gas-lit evenings sitting
bowed and cross-legged, with

the wings he'd like to make seamless
spread across his knees, shapely as an
ovaloid, wrap-around map
of the world. He is

redefining boundaries; he's
as dexterous as Leonardo
whose cagey machines of wire
and string might have flown,

given the skill to construct them.
The tailor has stitched his wings himself –
he is a practical man
who's tired of being

human. He'll reach beyond the glass
ceiling of being Vitruvian:
the sky's the limit. He stands –
fidgeting slightly –

on the tower, improbable
as *God, surrounded by fire with a
pair of compasses*; so high
the horizon's round

beneath his feet. But why will he
not jump? He surely can't doubt there is
any way out except up?
The sky looks heavy

enough to carry him; his wings
quiver as if they're ready to fly,
and of course the spectators'
faith will support him.

They know there must be wires, string or
at least a trampoline; there's no such
thing as *Disaster Today*.
So when he plunges

into his new element, black
and needle-fine as a cormorant
with his world-encompassing
wings pressed flat to his

back, they think what a fool he is
to have forgotten the trick. He has
broken the rules, and surely,
they think, in the face

of such idiocy there is
some last resort, surely by an act
of God the earth will open
and swallow him up?

# Ramona Herdman

## Falldown

Some of us are yet too scared
to take your pills like petals, wet
like the tip of a tongue on the tip
of the tongue.

We watch as you dance blind
tied to the falling trapeze
your hands only capable of holding
the cogs of your own knees.

We have warmed our palms
on the sweat and the open-eyed love
that you let fall like snowy fingertaps
from your foetal highs.

You know you'll fall down,
inevitable as the explosive letdown
of the tingle of the coming
of a sneeze.

You know you'll fall down
when you look down
when it wears off
when you start to care.

You know later
you'll need more touching

than stars hiccuping
in your hair.

Come down please.
We are earthbound.
We are manacled by our knees,
by our belief

in broken bones.
Come down to us,
to limits, bedtimes,
the small things of home.

Come down before you fall down*
because if you fall down
we'll never dare
step above our footstools,

root chair on chair
and rocket up, our footprints
corn circles, pebble-dabs on pools.
Whilst you are up

our necks are cricked.
To the depths of our ritual
corn and berry stomach-contents
we are sick.

Whilst you are up
the comet-tail of your comedown,
sharp as a lift-shaft,
wavers under you.

Whilst you are up
our palms
shiver like the ultra-violet
cups of caverned mushrooms,

white as the filament
in the unlit throats of doves,
they grab our arms up.
We wave ourselves like handkerchiefs

wanting you to drop.
When you're down we're both morose.
Fetid sweat of fear or hope
smells the same: dead mouse, too close.

O, when you're up
you're very very good.
You are white as a ringlet,
adorable, soft

as the incurl of a shell.
When you are elevated, manic,
sanctified,
I want to make you well.

Come down before you fall down.
Down the fall, so it's shot
like a clay pigeon
and I can see

its lack of threat –
crumble it like powder in my palm
and you can get
more pills.

The moment you're going up for,
that I'm staying down, coming
up with, is the instant
at the salt rim,

the lifted step, the shared bubble
of breath before the first kiss.

The moment when nothing is: the emptiness
that cannot fall.

Come down so you can be going up
slow as a feather, rooted in the
future imperfect, the middle syllable.
The perfect moment before it all.

* *This line first appeared in a poem by Ross Sutherland.*

## After the Ants

My kitchen smells of the killing of ants.
She'd said they were as big as killer bees
and she didn't want to kill them
just wanted them to leave.

The house has one too many mirrors.
The one downstairs is the sister
of the one over the bath.

They don't like me any more,
don't bother
with my good points
because they want the other woman back –
the one who smoothed my toothpaste spit.

They won't allow me to look clean.
In their views I am always in that scene,
my fingers black
as the burnt-sugar corpses of ants,
redhanded with not knowing what she wants.
Her in the background, not coming back.

They make my face at me
over their sinks, bruised with my own
soapy fingerprints.

# Andrea C Holland

## On Diane Arbus and her
### *Albino Sword Swallower at a Carnival*

Born under a surgical lamp like a spotlight:
transluscent skin, her eyes pale
and fluttering like sick birds. At school

this one stood in the shade of a sycamore tree
and blinked like an owl. Her classmates whispered
and jostled together, played *Red Light Green Light*,

afraid to touch her: a sugar mouse, a doll in the shop
window, fading. But in her room at home she read
books about Princess Bea and her magical powers,

Princess Bea and her long sunlight hair. She practised
in the yard and insects curled as they flew by, stunned
by the heat in her. This girl bought a trick sword

to swallow; this girl bought a trick sword and swallowed;
this girl swallowed her sword and its shadow
passed down her beautiful clear throat

like a sentence – a language of clarity
lost in the dark world outside.

## The Missing Letter

The last word is not
love or the equivalent
and then your name. Instead
an interruption, someone calls
your name and you put the letter
down; it slips between the worn green

cushions on the sofa. The ink is green
too, and already fading. The letter is not
noticed and so not recalled. The letter
is a small one and though equivalent
to not much more than a phone call
you have chosen to write me instead.

This is important because instead
of finishing it you get up from the green
sofa and when your son's school calls
to say *he is ill again, come now*, you're not
thinking of the letter or any equivalent
distraction, *my son*, you think, the letter

M for Marco appearing in the sky, the letter
M and Marco dancing over the road signs instead
of the names of places, M in headlights, or their equivalent
tail-lights as cars rage by. The traffic light is green
but you don't go anywhere; you cannot
take your foot off the brake. Horns call

out like love-sick frogs. And when you call
his name walking through the school doors, the letter
M disappears, Marco is not
there. Someone suggests the hospital instead
and panic like quicksand, like a green
swamp rises in your chest. There is no equivalent

for the fear. For this fear there is no equivalent.
Fear like drowning. From the hospital phone calls
must be made, people need to know. The green
sofa hides an unfinished letter
which is found by your sister who, instead
of joining you offers to clean the house. She is not

able to say the equivalent of your words, if the letter
had been completed by you, so she calls me instead
to explain. She puts it in a green envelope and sends it. Or not.

## The Reluctant Bridegroom

When the Minister told me to place my ring
   on your third finger, as you had done mine,
your hand withdrew a little, a gesture
   of uncertainty as if my hands were hot
to the touch. As if testing a griddle
   or an electric fence. You probably thought
it was the wrong time for the ring to go on,
   that I was off cue. You pulled back your left
palm as if bitten. Your eyes said, *wait*.
   Our guests, the merry congregation, all laughed
like it was planned: part of the celebration, this joke
   – *I know, I'll take back my hand and make them wonder.*
But I implore you then, now, give me your warm palms
   and their slim digits like a comet with its trails.

You don't have to direct me, just give me your hand.
   Once on your skin, the rose gold beneath the white
surface of the ring: the pale red warm as an oven
   just turned off, or my heart when you are gone, pale.
The cooked metal has worn the flesh beneath your finger
   into a hard yellow whorl, and so you are marked,
as I am marked. It is that which holds you to me
   when you take this ring from your finger and commit it

to a box. It is your private celebration, the ceremony
   of letting go which you now choose. Husband, it's true:
I was always slightly off cue, I had trouble
   with the stars. Take my ring: wear it or don't.
It is the boundary around my heart, the circle
   around some distant moon which follows you
when you take another's hand. An electric fence
   humming in the dark under a congregation of stars.

## Mayday

A grimace from the spine and my belly
pouts. My load leads me forward
like a figurehead on the ship's prow,
a garish girl painted thick to keep out
the water's rot. She's sure there's a shore
somewhere, an unlocated island with a dry dock
and the long effort of unloading cargo,

a relief. But the voyage goes on under
dizzying stars, not comforted by longitude
or familiar seas. Navigation, longshoreman,
can I give up the goods or will I snap
like wet rope; unravel under strain? Or topple,
sink, cantilever into sargasso green, mast
split in two.

The painted girl's fierce eyes glaze over, dulled.
Fishes swim to the stiff body slipping
from the bow, frozen forward, still in
motion, staring through the dark water
to a port now close at hand. But she's going
down, sinking like a sick shark; a dying
mermaid who cannot see the crowning

of this small Neptune; he who undid her,
swimming safely to the peopled shore.

# Matthew Hollis

---

## The Wash

All summer the rainfall was biblical.
Seawater, nightly, brought gifts to our door –

crab claws and hawser, a boat on the high street,
roads leading into the sea.

Each day the reach had been rising
and those who had seen it before

were talking of *waterslain* –
a flooding so surely as nightfall

sweeping a coastline to sea.
We filled the car with what we could –

our two cats, that pair of clocks,
heads awash with flood-lore –

who put the kerf on Friary roof;
who lost his wife but not one single book.

And, for a moment, it's upon us –

*We have taken the boat to the river,*
*toggled a path to the edge of the water*
*and put down where trout shoehorn at our feet.*
*In this boat bellied with paintpeel and moss*

I will guide us up river, away from the flood,
with a sackful of things clutched up
in the hours at dawn.

And husbands will call to their children
to come in off the field, come in
and wash for their tea. And they'll come
kell-faced and scrambling stories
of water, great water, climbing the hill.

And wives will flight from their fishing boats
smelling of rockwind and kelp
and stand ashen, ashen; or plashing
through rooms with sandbags and peat sod
scooping up kids from the runnels.

There will be no maps for where we are,
but a swirl of haybale, splints of timber,
cattle bloating in the current.

And later, much later,
the water will come from all sides at once
and our boat will welter and coup.

And in that moment I will hold you under.
Your face will moon from the water.

*

I have seen it inside you,
                              a cue ball

where part of your head should be.
You carry the thing sewn up in your skull

the sound of the sea trapped in
and trickling through shunts;

if you opened your mouth
seabirds would peck out your tongue.

You have sat with a friend who has it too
in cigarette clouds and silence;
                              and yet
nothing rhymes with cancer –
and this strange company is no company at all

but a waiting room of small arrangements –
the saltings turning with aster, samphire;

the shoals of Thief Sand, Black Buoy Knock;
the boats spilling their nets off the Staithe,

a shale of oysters, lobster pots,
mussels torn out of the creek.

Tonight I scoop you from an empty bath,
naked as whale bone,

                       left high on the tide,
and know by now what it is.

It's not the flood I fear but what comes after –
the endless roaming to find a home

like Shuck, the Viking dog, who beats
by legend a nightpath over these marshes

looking for a boat that's long pulled out,
to find place in the heart of nothing.

# The Stoneman

*A type, mind, is a little man;*
*a face, a beard, shoulders and arms,*
*look – even the shank of a body.*
             – A. R. Spalding, *The Mannerisms of Type*

I

A true navigator, he could course
the old print works from memory –
decoding a world of picas and rubies,
of going to the case for brevier, bourgeois;
lining the back-to-front type, sort by sort,
or leading the galley for the optimum gauge;
before taking the chase to the stoneman
who'd dress it with furniture, sidesticks, quoins,
measuring the gutters, and locking the forme for press.

A world of infinite detail, he learned
to tell founts by the slightest flourish:
the kern of an f, or the spur on a G –
those stubby descenders of *Goudy*;
those *Baskerville J*s, *Fournier z*s,
and the crazed swash of *Caslon*, *Garamond*.
He would scour the cases for dog's cocks, ampersands,
the Old Face of *Blado–Poliphilus*;
drumming up scraps on the origins of *out of sorts*,
or how we take *upper* and *lower* case
from the height at which the type was stored.

To handle the language like that –
to lift, assured, each letter into place,
knowing it either clean or dissed
(one or the other, no in-between);
and throwing the frocked type for the recast
when the paraffin no longer did the trick.

And yet, more than aware of composing a line
that would soon be lifted and distributed,
so that nothing he worked would survive him
only its residue: imposed, in print, out of it.

In the same way, his men are scattered now, far flung
or melted down, leaving only the legacy:
of how as a young devil some wag would send him
for skyhooks, striped ink, an italic space,
or the old long weight. And what after all
did the o say to the 8, but *I like your belt.*

2

'The, ah, thing, you know,
that goes with the mongoose,
no, mouse, no. Ah.'
                              Again.
'The thing, *this –*'
(triangular shape w. hands)
'and the thing, *this –*'
(rectangular shape w. hands)
'and I want some. Okay?'

Far from okay, it's November
and you've talked this way since March –
raffling for nouns, what my compositor
would call a pie, all out of sorts,
your galley of the swapped-around.

THANK            :                        GOD
how it makes you smile to hear yourself say
that you've fed the briefcase or the mantelpiece;
and, in its way, how eloquent that
booting your laptop 'manufactures the sky'.

But you're tongue-tied, belted,

deported from language, to where
'there are almost no zooms', or 'orange nosebags';
going to the place of 'the three easy ones',
the 'head-grind tea', or some such else;

and five miles out of surgery, your head still newly sown –
'When will the stonecutter come to cut the stone?'

3

Let me set this line the way you want it,
and lay the letters you would choose –
no damaged characters or battered type
no sort in need of planing;
no widows & orphans but the right fount:
sheer measure, aligned, and no omissions.

All we want is to draw a little proof from the world;
from time to time, catch sight of ourselves
in the printer's mirror and say we set it right,
before moving on to the stoneman
to leave his indelible mark;

so that long after the inking
and the distributing of sorts
what is left is binding, an impression, and paper.

## Passing Place

In the year before the year
before you died
we threaded our Ford

rainward –
foot by foot
up through the pass

of the Brecons,
tuning out of the radio
and all known language.

We were leaving England
on a car-width
cut out of the bluff

slewing back
for the pass
scooped into the hill

or rolling a wheel
on the hummock
and bog

at road signs
we could
no longer decipher.

But then language
was digging,
you would say,

going down
for the good words
which lay

just under the tongue –
not in phrase books
or schoolrooms

but the mor
and mull
of the language –

the loam of ourselves
tilled over,
grown in.

All day we went back
for the siding,
for the wide road

for the strange
communion
of each car by –

hand after hand
held up
to mine;

all day, back
for the road signs
ringing the cwm –

the PASSING PLACE
and what it was
in Welsh.

There are places
at which we stop,
pearl white

the rain in our mouth,
where we leave
language behind.

MAN PASIO.
As if we could
translate.

# Helen Ivory

## Just Words

We made sentences
out of odd phrases, you and I.
Clumsy structures
that let the rain in.

We built whole
philosophies
on foundations
of air and words alone.

Strange syntaxes
like translated English,
all back to front
and upside down.

And to think
this was our only tongue
when now the words
are chalk dust on my hands.

Particles fall silent
to the ground, as in a dream
or an old photograph,
lightly foxed.

## Clocks on the Rocks

The past is a thing of the past
said the man clocking his stopped watch.
There is only now and it is six o'clock.
He had checked his watch so many times in the past,
more times than he cared to remember.
Times when time was important,
when he had to be somewhere, somewhen ago.

He decided that six o'clock would be p.m.,
because six in the morning was always too early for him.
Six in the evening, home from work,
gin and tonic, ice and lemon. Perfect.
The ice cracks as it melts, and outside,
the gin-pink sun rocks steadily around its own clock.

## Note to the reader: this is not a poem

The pictures are falling from my walls
because the paint is too heavy.
Illusionary landscapes are real landscapes now.
No need for tonality, or warmth of colour.
Now I write another poem that nobody will read.
There is loneliness in these words.
I tell you, the non-existent reader in plain terms.
There is no need to hide behind poetry.
I won't try to be clever with you.

# David Allen Lambert

### origami whale

I could fold this paper
with delicate precision
creating curves from stiff straight edges
prompting you to ponder
how the paper could possibly be untorn?
and then you'd realise
you're holding a whale

yet I choose not to crease the paper
but to decorate it with memory

how a dark shape surfaced
huge and alive directly under the yacht
a warm-blooded secret amidst the waves' shadows
gentle despite the demanding deep

the whale ascended so close to our stern
it plunged immediately to avoid collision
no dramatic plume of moist breath rent the air
just a circle of water calmed by a careful fluke

transfixed I reached over the rudder
and stroked the smooth surface
my fingers rippled a fluid window
through which you and I now peer
distracted by our own reflections

## stars on a swing

on the hill overlooking
the night lights of the city
you and I invoke
the spirit of the child

we find a wall where we sing our fear
one hundred feet up from death
dancing on just two hands' width of concrete
never the world so wide

near by, a playground, and swings!
my legs shoot towards the sky
and if I pull my hands back
arch my neck like a bird about to fly
for an instant I am weightless
with nothing in my ears but laughter
and nothing in my eyes but stars stars stars

## faith's return

looking heavenward the fool lifts
a clueless step over the abyss

the stars enchanted by their reflections
upon such an unwavering gaze
extend the edge of creation

# Sarah Law

## Vampire in Therapy

It's the cold I'm always trying to escape from.
It seeps from my fingers and makes mice gasp.
I squeeze them, enraged by their purse of warmth,
the bloody oil slickening my nightrags, tight
as if I'm about to rent these threads.
You see, I'm a user, roaming in a pack
of unfriendship, wondering where the next
open neck, staggered collar, might wash
the fight down. The fear like eyes of ice.

What is normality? you ask, fingering your tie.
I see it all right, the blush on your skin,
the surge of empathic recoil, my self from myself.
Parents! They knew what they did, closely
guarding the age-old tortures, familiar, fusty,
missing all the light. Its rhythm, flex – I crave
illumination. More than blood. And you can help:
you the screen, the template, marbled horrors
of my own that flash and fade on this lucent palm.
You smooth me into curve of flesh, until I fit
my waking world. My own blue pulse and orb.

## On Stuffing, Roasting and Eating a Chicken After Half a Lifetime of Vegetarianism

Puckered flesh is yielding its dismemberment
as, hands scrubbed clean and raw, I'm spooning
hot stuffing – sage and thyme – into cavities.

Sam takes a photo: two young ladies, alone
for the festive season, abandoning decades
of unparalleled green leaves, for mischief, meat.

Odd how familiar a ritual this is, harking back
to the laid-down foundations of childhood,
the slip of the skin, the containment of death
into nourishment, nurture, the consistency of things.

Roasting for so long – she calculates the pounds –
we get the snuff of grandmotherly kitchens,
that grease on the hands, the warming of plates.

It's transgressional, for us, but life holds softly
the vagaries of spinster saturnalia, laughing
at ourselves, the mesh of unsung carols, chords
and speculative steps. The oven's secured
with nutcrackers.

In good time, we claim and carve
dinner: a faint lake of blood settling in the dish,
the clink of our glasses over a living stream.


## What Is the Sound of One Hand Clapping?

It is the sound of paradox and cliché. Lying
in the yoga class at end of play, it is the clinch.
It has been stretched for years and needs a rest.
It is the sound of the air on your face, air that has swirled

round the school gym, while the poses swung and held.
It is the sound of ceaseless, futile effort.
It is the glide of flexed and silent ease.
It is the muted wave of one who lacks a catch,
the simple mind that lacks a voice.
It is the slap of palm on thigh, mass applaud
as the class warms up by Chinese massage.
It is the slight, half-hearted politesse
of those whose half-time drinks are full and precious.
It is the soundless rage of prisoners,
the careful patting of the sly, the subtle sleight
of the master detective, seeking hidden doors.
It is skin folded in, and then extended,
a swift flamenco clip. A grasp of sand:
a koan half dissolved, and half in hand.

## The Baroque Netter

lies quietly, his instruments to hand. This
hand is the only part of him exposed
to the moted warmth of bedroom elements.
Forearm disguised as a branch, hand pale and splayed
as if it should be rooted in the earth, or
flexing over keyboard, food, and flesh.
Instead, he stays ready, finger poised
to net the prize of music on demand, as
it flows, swift, silver through the channel
of transmitted time. The real trophy
is Bach. He is the stream
of treasures without end. And this the year
richer than others ever shall have been.
The wise, insistent tones, the crystal fugues
nose their way through stations on the dial,
and are diverted into reels of tape. The man,
as master poacher of the waves, waits, silent
until he hears the herald of their play.

Then, pressing down the buttons, feels the slide
of counterpointed shoals safe at his side.
The catch provides sustenance, easing pressure
as a disjointed world jangles over the sheets.

## Diagnosis of a Mystic
*based on the life and migraines of Hildegard of Bingen*

*I saw a cedar planted on an egg*
*and round it was a shimmering of faith.*
This vision took me to my bed. Stiffly
I lay, denying all new truths,
adhering to the rules of my girlhood,
when I was taken in. These kindly nuns
live a sober life, but told me tales
of mysteries, of saints, of martyrdoms;
Saint Catherine on the deadly spinning wheel,
Saint Agatha who lost her lovely breasts,
another saint who sang, even when her throat was cut,
I liked this saint – Cecilia – the best.
At night, her silver tones enwrapped my body,
galvanising prayer, supple, self-spun.

I grew into a habit.

*Flaming threads, premonitory birds,*
*bright petals flashing in a breeze,*
all these I saw. And ripping through the mind
an aching blade. The devil in the raw.

I could not think that I should come to good,
yet heal I must: both others and myself.
I studied states of woman and of man –
their cyclical disorders, muscle spasms,
dread and marvel close behind, as angels
of watchfulness, tenderness, trained
my hand. This was a precious time.

*Dark the chapel, pealing with distress*
*as ribbons moulded phsyick unto death*
*and though my brow was gored, my voice*
*cried 'Yes' – let lightpoints blaze*
*where no light was –*

My sinews tautened in anticipation
of further pain. My flesh dried up,
my neck in constant tension, ears and eyes
poor, sore servants of the Holy One.

But stand – and dance – I did.

I was struck high     with blows of ecstasy

untrammeled flares          of otherworldly gleam

a holocaust     of understanding scrolled back from a dream

I saw the stars     fly into darkest shade

the sun enlarged               enclosing all things made

and all my sisters     clad in lily white     with golden crowns

I saw them gather round. I heard them sing.

*I am a feather on the breath of God.*

I loved a sister once; she cared for me
the way I wish I could have cared for all.
She left this sorry world.      I still remain.

I live to paint and sing my visions out,
though it shall kill me.
Wise men travel here; I counsel kings.

The One I serve enfolds my head in fire,
the better to illuminate Her ways;
I am a feather, fibrillating, dazed,
I sing through severance.
I am amazed.

# Julia Lee

---

## Ben Lomond

*for Matthew*

My thighs are burning and I am bathed in sweat,
I am over-reaching myself.
My eyes see pine trees and my feet feel stones.
I am swimming through the wet, sticky heat.
My steps beat litanies onto the path:
*I was a fool to take this on*
*so like me so always like me*
*I am on a treadmill I cannot leave*
*I am not strong I have never been strong.*
Suffering now suffering
too much to think anything else;
clearing the sweat from my forehead
licking my lips, swallowing the dry swallow of someone
                                        conserving water
*– through all this your soft lips sustain me –*
unable to think of this as over,
measuring time merely as steps
and all directions, all perceptions to one thing,
which is more.

## Untitled

Don't lose your hat
don't leave it behind
with me.

Don't leave your hat
to sit judgement on me,
the hanging judge
a little death each time I pass.

## You Mean You Don't Have Autumn in Vietnam?
*for Thoa*

See, how the trees turn to flame –
no, sorry, that's an English cliché,
yes, I know, another one,
I've been in a forest fire,
scariest moment of my life,
so that, I know damn well,
is not trees turning to flame.

But if you look again, actually,
at the way they're going red around the outside
and yellow on the inside and kind of
marching across the countryside –
are you getting any of this? –
they look a bit like flames,
like God's fire made on our hillside.
And the shape, of course.
Well, maybe the shape's feathers. I don't know.

Why? I don't know why.
I knew in primary school. Maybe.
I mean, you're the ecology student.
Well, yeah, I know you mostly do mangrove,

and you don't have deciduous –
de-cid-u-ous trees in Vietnam,
but I don't know anything about trees.
Autumn? Well, it just happens.
Always has done.
And you know what?
Look, here's a leaf pile.
It's traditional to jump up and down in them.
Listen! Listen! Skoosh! Skoosh!
You know what it reminds me of?
Reminds me of the rice paper you used when you taught me to
                                      make spring rolls.

# Joanne Limburg

## The Making of an English Poem

This is one of those English poems
which begins with the mating
of two ideas.

The first idea arrived in Kremenchug,
perhaps in the mind of the poet's great-grandmother,
as she hid with her daughters in the yeasty darkness
of her husband's bakery ovens,
waiting for the cossacks to ride away
and wondering, in Yiddish, how long could they stay here –
for all that it was home, how long?

A family friend tipped them off
about the second idea,
written in Russian, officially stamped,
rolled up in the fist of a secret policeman
who had some questions for the poet's great-uncle
regarding the Student Revolution.

The Yiddish idea met the Russian idea,
they sparked and fused.
The family wrapped the poem up, in its loose first draft,
along with the poet's infant grandmother
and so began its long, uncomfortable voyage
towards the English page.

As with so many poems,
the middle stage of its making was the hardest,
a stumbling night's journey
full of accidents and wrong turns.
The plan to write an American poem
was scuppered by an unscrupulous captain
who assured the poet's great-grandfather
that a Humber lighthouse was the Statue of Liberty;
then the poem nearly choked in its attempt
to assimilate the legalese
of the Alien Immigration Act.

Once a poem has survived its crisis,
it only remains to tidy up the language.
The poem settled in Whitechapel,
where it went to school with the poet's grandmother,
acquiring at her side
a native's English and an East End accent.

After that, a little pruning,
to edit out the gutteral sounds and jerky rhythms
which would otherwise disfigure
our English poem.
When the poet's mother received her degree,
it collected a set of BBC vowels,

then joined its poet, for a final polish,
at her private school and Oxbridge,
where it became this English poem:
so laconic, so understated,
so *decent*, you'd never know
the poet's family weren't washed up
with the Vikings, the Normans or the Huguenots.

## Nonsense Wedding

Congratulations, Bride-to-Be!

You've made your first selection –
the bridegroom.
Now you can leave the rest to us.

We'll whip your special day
into a perfect dream.
We'll float you through our showroom
on a carpet of petals and someone else's money.

Our complete package includes
complimentary use of all oxygen
on our premises,
co-ordinated weather
and removal of all stains from your past.

We'll arrange the guests you choose
into pairs and family groups,
every one a charming set
wrapped up in a shiny box,
delivered on the day.

Then there are those personal touches.
Why not have the bridesmaids monogrammed?
Dye your mother's eyes to match your shoes?
Issue each guest with porcelain teeth
for perfect photographs?

We can even have the waiting staff
shrunk, preserved
and delivered to all your guests
in special presentation boxes –
the perfect souvenir
of a day they'll love to remember!

And when your special day is over
we'll deliver you home
to your personal box
where you can treasure each other forever,
you perfect couple, you matching set.

Allow us to wish you the best of luck –
we hope you'll always shop with us!

## Maurice Limburg's Dream

In the recurring dream
I share with my late father,
the stars whirl in the sky
like reflected lights
in stirred black coffee.

If we think of his brain
and mine
as two soft machines
built from one blueprint,

then this dream
must be a stored programme,
hardwired into identical circuits,
a wholly transmittable,
ineradicable file,

so that every time
the stars whirl in my sleep,
there's an open file
marked *Maurice Limburg's Dream*,
as I run the programme
made of thoughts
that made my father.

# John McCullough

## PVC Trousers

make you creak when you walk.
Try to hide that from your father.
Try to hide that from the taxi driver
who looks like your father.
Hide it with a coat, laughter.

Let loose at the club
pretending you're naked, shameless.
Pretending they're not the first
thing on your mind.
That you're walking not strutting.

Have your arse squeezed,
legs smoothed.
Spill a pint.
You're waterproof.

You seem too perfect.
Make sure you speak
of the sweat, the tautness,
your father.

Wear them again next week.

## Kimono

I wake to strange sheets,
the insistence of rain.
The easy strength of your hum:
well-established, at home,
following white hands through
a green wardrobe.

You turn, smile, and present today's clothing
as last night whispers itself in snatches:
stubble, your aftershave, a taxi ride back.

The kimono is black, embroidered
with orchids in pink.
Its cool silk slides round my ribs,
slinks my wrists like a suit of water.

I sit back and listen,
pull the cord tauter.
Somehow I feel smaller than yesterday:
cat-size.

You laugh and bring milk,
feed me toast and fried eggs.

A print of James Dean
hangs over the bed,
throws back my inertia
in black and white terms
with one low-swung cigarette.

I roll and breathe slowly
into the pillow,
the most princely dead thing
aware only of rain.

The silk is lifted,
falls round my hips.
I close stately eyes
and tense for the kiss.

## Liar

You smoke too much:
scrubbed fingers keep
the saffron sheen
of forty years of inhalation;
like onion skins in iodine
under a microscope.

You won't fool me
with that rinsed air
of openness today
as we collide in the pub
nearest your house:

small face, mouse-like;
whatever glance it sends
I know – I've seen you
with your friends:
the mafia of the bowling alley.

Scorsese moment when
you turfed an old couple
out of your lane,
your voice a false jumble
of guttural vowels.

I know all I'll get from you
is two hours, a Fosters.
Not bitter – I understand
the point of armour,
your oxygen masks.

The magician who only wears
ropes he can slip from
(though unluckily, Dad,
you're not especially fast).

## Ebury Way

Run back to Christmas ten years ago,
feet thumping red wellingtons over the bridge.
Squelch of rubber on concrete, ears naked and brittle,
the river iced over, tea-coloured,
                                no fish.

A dog round my heels, head bursting the air.
My comrade behind, catching us at the stile
as we fall into a field of stiff, bristly grass.
His smile unexpected, just over his scarf.

The night has left vast icy puddles,
cheap gifts we open rudely, with feet,
smash into clean blades we pick up
and throw back.

I look up into his eyes
as we smash, feel the cool rush
of the cold through the sides of my boots,
the dog lapping the water up quickly, wincing.

Ebury Way. I didn't know that
was its name till last year

when they put up the signs:
white letters on blue.

Ebury Way. My lips stumble the *b*.
Not resentful but always again
unexpecting, still fresh to the water,
                                    burying.

## Mr Shell

even the litter lies compliant
folded, stored within white bags
within blue bins
smell of detergent and fresh-baked cake

in the long vase the bought lilies
stand uncluttered
a tea towel hangs precise
there is no washing up

though the sky may fall
milk is tidy in the fridge
and the curved stools stand
stock: grins on legs

in the corner stands Mr Shell
quiet as the knives
'just another utensil'
he'd like you to say

his eyes follow the breeze
to the newly mown lawn
to a spade which has lain by the shed
unused for the past five years

he'll put it away

# Andrew McDonnell

## Dead Girl on the Kitchen Floor

A first glance and it seems she is submerged in bathwater,
her hair flowing out behind her, her mouth curled by pleasure,
then you notice the broken wine glass in her left hand,
its contents spreading out, as if a child's blowing through a
                                                            straw,
the contents red, there can be no other colour.

She is more beautiful than anything else in the world, lying in
                                                    her stillness,
she is somehow complete, somehow picture perfect,
you can feel her breath run down the back of your neck,
she is your Cleopatra, she is your Queen of Sheba, she is your
                                                    Helen of Troy,
yet you don't know her, you've never met her, but you're
                                        reflected in her dead eyes.

There's a subdued happiness in your heart, a slow burning
                                                        curiosity,
if you put your ears to her mouth, you can still hear her singing,
singing your name, through blue pursed lips, like murmurs
                                                under bathwater,
and in your brain, there is Christmas tree lights twinkling, her
                                        head in every bauble,
reflecting a warped, *not quite right*, image of perfection.

And there is this lasting nagging silence, growing in your central
                                                              core,
it's untouchable, like distant lights as you travel on a motorway
                                                          at night,
she is dead, but not quite dead, she is somehow obtainable,
and her invisible silent words fall like snow upon your face,
for she knows your darkest thoughts, and will always carry them
                                       with her on her journey.


## From the Throat

One hundred thousand voices,
fall from my tongue,
conspiring in shadows that did not exist ten years before.

(She has been up in her basket blacking out the stars.)

Conspiring with one hundred thousand voices,
spilt from a waitress in a coffee shop,
onto a china plate, decorated by a rose.

(My mother's plates were the same, I watched them through a
                                       glass donkey.)

I can hear only one voice, it vibrates from a fleshy interior I do
                                       not fully understand,
others can hear several, ears of corn, smell of hair,
echoes of perfume from alien bodies, tea stains screaming.

(I see daffodils in a vase, think of my father's office, agricultural
                                       coasters, agricultural calendars.)

Some voices say to me: 'Mr McDonnell', I wait for my father
                                       to answer
and a million images cascade through my mind, dene holes in
                                       snow, Eynsford ford.

In my father's voice, I will answer 'Yes', but to them my voice
is strong, assured even.

(I think of a urinal at Goodwood, aged 4, hearing the sound of
hooves hammering the turf.)

Here, where everything ends for a passing moment, and I lie in
someone's arms,
and they whisper through my hair, words without voice, with
careless lovable force,
it is all laid to rest, and I sleep, and I rest and I rest and I rest . . .

(I'm in a flat that should be a gallery, pushing a cot tied with
helium balloons into a grey empty sky.)

## The Cream TV Set and the Eucalyptus Trees

The telegraph poles stretch to the sunset,
where the blazing days end,
coats everything in the deepest red,
and you can pick out a motel,
where a faded rainwater Virgin Mary stares at the emptiness,

and in room 27, a night-dress and a long coat dance,
the people inside them lazily drunk,
they have been this way for hours, not seeing the other's face,
she keeps trying to catch their reflection in the dusty cream
television set,
he runs his hands ever so slowly, over every inch of her back,
searching for a dip, curve, or even just a mole, to remind him of
a girl called Madeline.

As always human beauty collapses in on itself,
the sun finishes painting the eucalyptus
the relentless buzz of strip lights, start to him in the night,
and the drunken lovers have fallen asleep against each other,
while the stars overhead glitter half-heartedly in the western sky

# Lee McNicoll

## Closed

I am lacing up my eyes,
So that I cannot see you.
I am buttoning my mind,
So that you cannot enter.
I am zipping up my heart,
So that you cannot touch it.
But what I want
What I need
Is for you to undo me.

## Stars

We can smell the darkness,
taste the night's saltiness,
and so we appear.

While we are suspended,
shining upon your planet,
we can feel your stare.

Our light extends like creepers,
as we reach to your bodies,
touch your cold cities.

We remain so quiet,
whispering over clouds,
shuffling through mist.

We feel you gazing,
stretching for our tiny forms,
we hear your exhalations.

And so come the wishes.
Feeding our insides,
floating in our tiny bellies.

And we hold them silently
examine them carefully
return them dutifully.

Through these wishes we know you,
as you pray to us,
yet we are powerless,

pinned against a heavy sky
voices reduced to a whisper
(or so we say).

## Babyface

How could you know
what it feels like
to have the insides
of your sweating body
torn out right before your eyes?

And the screaming.
I was calling as loud as you were,
in the place where you were,
But the gloved hands

reached towards
your tiny frame.
I was left crying.

And later,
when I dressed you,
pushed your tiny arms,
flesh soft and pink
smell of marzipan,
down the woollen tunnels of a cardigan,
I could have kept on pushing,
stuffing the knitted top
until you vanished.

You cannot imagine
how it felt
when your cries battered at my ears,
the night shattered by your scream.
How my body felt stitched into my bedding,
Why I covered my ears.

You would not look at me.
Your soft head set against my shoulder,
my fingers loathed to touch you.

When walking in silence,
pushing your metal pram,
how my heart ached
at the mothers around us.

You could not imagine
how my heart ached.

I cannot explain
how I hate myself.

## E.T.A.

Headlights slice through
the blackness,
fat metal bodies driving
without thought,
the rotation of pitted wheels
a thousand oblivious
turns per minute.

Roadside verges blur
into a continual
slick of green,
the car churning forward,
your eye fixed to the road
like the gleaming cat's eyes
which hypnotize you.

White markings
merge into one long line,
drawing you,
pulling you,
your eyelids closing,
neck flopping like a broken doll.

Then the moonlight
throws itself upon
the smooth line of your windscreen.
You screw your eyes.
A footprint on the inside
of the passenger's side,
smeared and shining,
reflecting on your skin,
toe prints dancing
in your mind

where once again
our twisted bodies
rub. Clambering.
Feet pressed tight
against the icy sheath
of the window.

Warm breath rubbing
like tongues against
the glass. Frosted.

Scrape through condensation with
trembling finger.
Bodies clinging. Clawed.

Back arched. Small pebbles
of your spine rippling. Black
leather seats. Tiny beads of sweat
resting in pits. Fast.

Hairs erect. Palms spread
against the solid dashboard.
Nipples hard. Sucked.

Your breath staggering.
Humming engine driving
through your veins.
Eyes flashing like headlights.
Adrenalin at the clutch.

Then the clouds hide
the frosted cheeks of
the waxing moon,
the footprint retreats,
your mind vacated,
vehicles grind past you,
cars churning forward,
and its lack of reflection,
absence of shadow,
nothing, Nothing,
Headlights.

# Kona Macphee

## Hugh's Boomerang

A haze of eucalyptus oil
in sun-fermented vapour dazes
khaki trees to blue

and lubricates the air; a hunting
boomerang slips through it, winging
skew as a drunken fruitbat,

its barely slowing *whuh whuh whuh*
two coarse-thewed copter blades come loose.
A hunter's lethal spiral

is spun here to a tourist's toy
skimming the foreign green of trees
that know a leaner sun.

(O land of subtle colours, land
of larger air, you cannot catch:
I was not cleanly thrown.)

## Three Poems

## 1. Ice

1

Cold blue morning. Tiles of ice are laid
with perfect fit to puddles, frost
unhides the webs that chill-curled spiders made.

The tiny spikes on prickleweeds are flossed
with water crystals, grasses dusted
white with weather; footprints are embossed

along the path where treading broke the crusted
membrane of the night. Afloat
and lambent, fragile particles are mustered

to dance the clouds of breath that clear my throat.
Sunrise slices like a blade
and severed hoarfrost flecks my overcoat.

2

On promising evenings the weatherman said
the night would be freezing, so just before bed,
every winter, once or twice,
we filled a saucer and hoped for ice.

*Every winter, once or twice,*
*We filled a saucer and hoped for ice.*

We never had sleet, we never had snow,
and frost was rare and quick to go,
but every winter, once or twice,
we filled a saucer and hoped for ice.

*Every winter, once or twice,*
*We filled a saucer and hoped for ice.*

And early next morning we'd check the saucer
and always find it was filled with water,
yet every winter, once or twice,
we filled a saucer and hoped for ice.

*Every winter, once or twice,*
*We filled a saucer and hoped for ice.*

3

Through years as blue as sea-ice, striped
with white-thick scars (the cracks that healed
unevenly), observe the scene:

the schoolbag, gymslip, spider-plant
still green (that browned before Grade Two
and died), the Snoopy toy, the puzzle

pieces garbled round the floor,
the half-light seeping through the gap
between the frame and drawn-to door,

the cheeks crushed in his canetoad hand
to mouth a goldfish 'o' (a pout
for him to push his fat prick through):

a picture under glass. And now
a season's silence runs its course.
The sun has risen. Start the thaw.

## 2. No Fairy Story

I don't need to tell you what you've done;
I'm sure your memory opens at the thumb
to its favourite page, its pathetic glory:
the centrefold smuggled in a bedtime story.

You played Red King to my Unhappy Princess
and stowed your secrets beneath my mattress:
they kept me awake to the menace of your tread
and mocked the underpants I always wore to bed.

And what can Happy Ever Afters do
when every time I think I've banished you
your thumb slips in and prises me apart,
a staple through my abdomen, another through my heart?

## 3.

I give you words as fierce as fire
I give you voice as heard as ear
  o child –
    my great grief
    my held mute

I give you rooms as new as air
I give you dreams as safe as near
  o child –
    my tight sheaf
    my hard fruit

I give you stop as last as pyre
I give you then as far as fear
  o child –
    my too brief
    my point moot

I give you heart as brave as dare
I give you love as rich as dear
   o child –
      my sole fief
      my deep root

I give you hope as high as spire
I give you home as close as here
   o child –
      my pressed leaf
      my green shoot

# Mary Macrae Gibson

## My Mother, Your Mother, Our Mother

Among the sirens
war withholds its peace
and is silent.
*My Bonny Lies Over the Ocean* we sing,
but no words dare the thin paper of distance
to bring her back.

A crowd, a pickaxe, and a cry.
One hot dusty death before the rest,
brought by long men in overcoats
to the unplayed spinet and the thin shadow of a cough.
Craven-A smoke surrounds the throbbing wireless,
expediting an exit.

You, peeping through exotic filigree,
watch gentle arms
cradle Jerusalem's pale defeat
up the Khan's ancient stairs.
The muezzin goes unheard,
as *Inshallah*, they murmur, not believing.
Thin words hush;
'Maman est fatigué, vas t'en.'

Dead Poches line your family vault
Olga, Marie, Rodolphe, Adolphe.
Her names are there,
*Violette*, in French. *Neé Scudamore*.

I and the others do not exist;
thin letters hammered into brass
have buffed away the halfway years
and left us stateless.

'My mother,' we say, and try again.
'Your mother,' our faces echoing the same blood
which runs in different courses in our veins.
You light another cigarette, and cough,
a cloudy glass of *arak* by your side.
'I do not know,' you say in French, 'I was too young.
They say Papa had always loved her, all Aleppo knew.'
I think of eggs hidden in an Easter garden;
apple water-ice bought at the gate;
smoke playing in thin drifts about my hair.
'Our mother,' I begin, and have to stop.
'I was too young as well,' I say.

## Remembering Ivy

I remember her eyes,
small sharp blackcurrants
jigging from side to side,
when I told her
about my aunt's parrot,
how the visitor wouldn't part with his hat,
what the maid found on the tray

I remember her lips,
pale thin plasticine
airtight against the seepage of mirth;
her grandmother's cameo brooch
in its seed pearl berth
rocking on its moorings

I remember her elbows,
needles of bone
knitting the thin sides
through the crocheted flowers
and whispered crêpe de Chine

I remember her fingers,
bent wood pea-sticks
ready to ensnare a laugh
should it escape

I remember her skin,
white tissue paper,
too thin to conceal her glee

I remember her dying,
the gust of joy which carried her away

## EHW, Forty Years On

He's in there somewhere;
the eyes
look out from smaller windows,
set back into walls of bone.
I search for a memory of his smile,
see a laugh, pipe held in hand,
hear Amaryllis, still in green,*
dancing down the years.
Well-heeled socks and shoes
speak of acceptance;
we talk of old friends, of gardening, of ringing swifts,
of music; music then and now,
of that time when everything happened
and nothing had started.
He's in there somewhere, I swear I caught a glimpse.

* 'Amaryllis Dressed in Green' is a madrigal by William Byrd.

# Neil Martin

## Gubbins

Outback fen way, beyond where
the ditch stops and the marsh starts,
a sameface in hollow oak sits

watching the water split into riddles
and east its way to the Wash
through silt muck and poisonous puddles.

His Christian name is Jim,
but we all call him
Marshman, what's-his-chops,

black-eyed bastard of the Boston docks.
Our piebald pidgin kid
covered in creosote and cuckoo spit.

He is autumn when the leaves have fallen,
a pure plain version of things
cooped up in that wiry shed

and inbred of yokel lore:
folk say he paints his glasshouse
and eats live chickens

and how many fingers are in those mittens?
those beetroot palms we pay to kill the kittens?
With a spine like a crooked spire

he stalks across Amberstick common
firking for the magpie metal on night fires
and yelping at council kids who scarper

behind streetlamps, into well-lit houses,
warning Neighbourhood Watch and stepdads
who scare him off with cricket bats.

Now our Jim's final fit still twitches
beneath the tip of a tin mountain,
blue as a robin's egg but for the hue

of two flaming turnips on his cheeks.
One pearl eye rolls into skull sky.
One cross-eye almost weeps.

## The Design Faults of a Volvo 850 Estate

Bank Holiday Monday and all the cars are waxed.

A pinkish man trawls a butterfly net
around his swimming pool, bobbing the yellow leaves,

whilst the gardener sweet-talks his wife
who is drying out in a midday blaze,

backfloating on rippled towels and factor five.
The children are always thirsty, cross-legged

beneath virgin pine or mesmerised
by the death-match of two wasps trapped in a honey jar.

Later, when the sprinklers have switched themselves off
and the sky has filled with lemon tea

she will fumble sundrunk out of a single slip
and dangle Chinese sandals from a limp wrist

as if late home from a night on the town.
She will confess to a string of affairs.

He will chain-smoke through the night,
pock-mark the sofabed and stub butts

into the broken belly of a porcelain pig.
Tinker with the transmission, fix the fanbelt.

She will count sheep, cry over holiday snaps,
kept awake by synchronised central locks

that yelp like dogs being kicked from their sleep.

## Ursa Minor

This is the time of night
when I might find you in my sleep,
dozing on a dead arm
or tugging my pyjama sleeve.

The first thing that I see
is the blink of your St Christopher
then the clockwise orbit of a torch
tethered to the crossbeam in your father's loft,

whirling the fluorescent dust
down to a touchable cosmos.
I think about the provisions we'll need:
a copy of *Ocean Symphony*, a thermos flask,

your dog-eared horoscope, some digestives.
We plump them under pullovers

and reach for the skylight, hitching ourselves up
through the warm snags of a swallow's nest.

It is a late and cloudless night,
perfect for moonbathing on the tiles.
The Great Bear stretches his limbs
above the chimney

and the constellations
come out in a shiver.
With a thumb light as lithium
you trace the flight path of a satellite

as it patiently defies the world's turn.
I swallow my Adam's apple upwards
and almost jump –

                but wake instead
to whale sounds floating around the fenlands,
the postman whistling sweet nothings.


## Home Turf

The crumpled note in my brother's fist
says 'Flat 4a, Witham Bank East'.
He knock-knocks the letterbox
and through a pear-glazed window

we watch an adopted alley cat
shrink beneath browning house plants,
surprised by us or drops of fresh Artex,
sloshed around the ceiling

in uneven brushstrokes.
And there is my father,
odd-socked, unready, but glad also,
rushing to the door in his blue kimono.

It is our first visit to his bedsit.
We plonk ourselves down on the leatherette
like footballers on a visitors' bench
and play a game of I-Spy:

coffee rings blot the only spare inch of trunk top,
junk mail looks to have been read
and a good round of Patience
stacks the family line into four neat rows.

Whilst he fusses around us
with beakers of Dandelion and Burdock,
we belch along to *Sgt. Pepper*
and count down the leccy meter

before it swallows the last of the small change.
Hand-puppets appear out of candle shadows on the wall,
panto dragons writhing above stacks of hardbacks
silhouetted like pagodas at dawn.

We laugh and find our own light
in the click-blink of the fridge door,
amazed at the sight of ourselves
squinting through sixty watts of silence.

It is late.
The test card wails down every channel
and a lone tumbler goes whirling
around the gramophone.

And there is my father,
laid-out in the topiary of tiny bonsai,
drunk in his underwear.
One free hand flaps noiselessly in mid-air.


## His Love of Words

He will sit for hours
doing the crosswords,
a chewed biro blotting
on the tip of his tongue
like a half-remembered phrase.

He might read
a difficult conundrum to the cat
or quiz the dictionary
laid open on the side-dresser,
shrugging its shoulders.

And some days pass
when he says nothing at all,
only the Lord's Prayer at his bedside
and the all-night mime
of eleven down's tricky lettering.

So many synonyms!
His elaborate, worked-at verse
just a roundabout way
of saying things. *Expression
of deep affection. Three words.*

# Anika Moje

## Summer, Friday Evening

The boy and his
father, both wearing
white tennis shoes,
leave the house,
a baseball glove
and a bowl of potato salad
in their hands.
The screen door
slams shut behind them,
and the mother's 'have fun'
still rings in the child's ears
as he climbs into the car.
This is daily life:
a constant leaving-behind,
a shifting of rooms
and slamming of doors,
always going places.

## Poem to Will Oldham

I imagine hills in Kentucky,
the place you might call home.
Rolling, lush and green.
Although I am not even sure
whether there are hills in Kentucky.

The one picture I have
of you, you are wearing
a straw hat and I imagine
you are holding a cigarette
in your hand, always smoking
and drinking, a regular hero.

The night you visited my town,
I was not there to put
my arms around you,
like I wanted to.
They told me you were
singing well that night,
wearing a red T-shirt.
And the straw hat.
And then, smoking
and drinking.

## Premonition

While she was lying
in a hospital bed,
my father and I
were hauling the boat in
and I was burning with fever.
Moments later we were sitting
at a table outside our hotel
and a waitress made me choose
between apple and cherry pie.

Sweat running down my eyes,
shaking with cold,
I tried forcing
pieces of pie
into my mouth.

He went inside
to make the phone call.
When he came back out
to deliver the news,
I was still holding
the fork in my hands,
shaking.

## A Day Spent Outdoors

After unloading the truck
you get on your bike,
leaving me to walk the trails,
a puzzle of wrong turns
spread out before me.

I know that one of them
will eventually lead me
to you, a short hello
while your bike
brushes past me
so close, it almost
touches my skin
(remember what you did last night)
and then again I am left alone
amongst the trees,
wandering aimlessly,
a sudden silence after
a rush of unspoken words.

When I finally arrive at the
clearing, light against light,
you are sitting
on the back of
your truck, waiting.

## Life Before Man

The first time we danced,
I almost crawled inside you,
curled up like a cocoon,
the warmth of your body
containing me.
I imagine that, years later,
they would have found us –
the girl nestled inside
a man's body, her fists pressed
together in an embryonic gesture,
content, complete.
They would name it
'The fossil of a single moment' –
a life would never hold that much.
We wandered from hotel to hotel
judging the music at each.
This was my way of playing for time –
I had never danced before.
Back at our hotel, home of the
white tiger, I filled up on cheap
Midwestern beer until the whole place lit up
and even the sounds of the slot-machines
were music, losing and winning, a sweetness.
Your hands lifted me off the chair
and pulled me onto the dance floor and
I felt your boy's body pressed hard against me,
your small frame just a temporary host,
almost too frail for what is inside,
what I feel every night when you hold me.
I kept my eyes open only long enough
to see the other guests' approval
then closed them, holding you, crawling inside you,
reduced to instinct, reduced to feeling.
This is what it must have been like,
this life, life before man.

# Jane Monson

## The Cupboard

*Boo-boo! Boo-boo!*
*Where the hell are you?*

My mother is tired of this game
and today I have changed the rules:
when she gives me back my name
I will give her back her daughter.

Until then,
I belong to a piece of the dark
in a box under a sink.

I am breathing in fear:
I have picked a place in which I cannot tell
if my eyes are open or closed,
and my skin is pressed so close to walls
that if I'm found
I may be stilled
and left to play for ever,
cramped and coloured in pain.

*Boo-boo, Boo-boo, come on darling.*

My name is Jane,
my name is Jane.

The sticky soles of sandals are outside me;
I turn headlong into her sigh
where the thin stripe of light
in between the doors
vanishes,
her hand reaching down towards me;
a mother's palm,
the other side of my face.


## Babysitting

A doll abandoned in the living room
lies face-down, inches away from a pillow:
she is Anna's plastic girl,
nameless, in a squandered wreck of toys,
and I am being paid to preserve
the mess and its mistress;
trusted to keep everything safe
and to leave her as I would want to find her.

This part of the city is badly lit,
and tonight the streets are blurred under water:
miles and hours of rain
tracing the cracks and the slabs,
feet slapping in and out of puddles,
hooded shapes tucked inside shelters,
scantily dressed figures crammed into doorways,
lumpy carrier bags against their chests.

Inside, a voice from a bed
counting to ten in the dark,
muffled under covers
and escaping from her open door
into the hall.

I look down to listen closely:
scattered over the tiles
are crescent droppings of hair,
young, red and unsplit
smiling up at me
from my feet.

At last the rain has outdone her,
put out the flame of little lungs,
and everything is still
as it was,
as it should be,
before I was trusted.

## Out of the Rain in Peterborough Cathedral

Beneath the chairs,
side-by-side-cut-to-fit
a shade of movement,
a black wind on the floor;
shadows turned to soot
and blown by the skirt
of an old woman's leaving.
She had come to shelter herself
and the choir was unexpected;
she didn't plan to sit through songs,
to her they're unwanted, like rain.

So with the breath of cloth
around her ankles,
she cambers her back
to the priest
and his voices;

sweeps the sound up
where it hums in the scaffolds,
fills the empty poles of metal:
industrial limbs of music
climbing up to God,
reminding us to look up
and forget about departing dresses,
about age that doesn't believe,
but it was her leaving
that turned shadows to soot
and songs into scaffolding,
and that's as good as it gets in here.

# Melissa Moore

## The Onion Thief

From the kitchen window she watches
the nervous peak of his back
dipping into the blue onion field.

The furious jut and tick of his elbows and
buttocks, as he wrings two out of the dust,
slopes back to the house, low as a dog,
lays them out on the butcher's block.

The blue onion stalks like blood in retreat,
twin moons in silk parachutes,
or huge, feverish eyes, missing nothing.

He watches as she cleaves them open,
tacky sweetness and smack seeping
out of the tight watermarks,
reaching first her eyes, then his.

## The Hat

This is the point
where I picture you on tiptoe,
leaning far over the hoary river,
thundering past.

In my mind I see
your eyes tight closed,
conjuring up your life
as it leaves your hand and spins.

You spin it high as cloud
and watch it go,
winking like a coin
in the gun-metal air.

It goes climbing, climbing,
slicing the river's shadow,
and the ribbon is flying out behind
like the tail of a kite,

and I do not see it stop
or where or if it comes to rest.

Just your hand
held out in front of you,
as if still connected
by some fierce, unbroken thread.


## Remembrance

There is a Kertész photograph of a line of men
marching between Lonié and Mitulen, 1915.
And though I know this photograph is taken in Poland,
I swear it is the same field
where you and I once free-wheeled
on hired bicycles, snaking between
acres of turnips and winter wheat.
It was early spring and had rained.
We could almost see the woods coming into leaf,
feel the sun growing stronger
as we rode along the track,
worn smooth by a hundred thousand feet.

And though I have never even been to Poland
I'm sure I know this field.
And I know the face of this one young man
who is turning back to Kertész,
with his cap pushed back off his forehead
and a rifle on each shoulder.
And although his boots are out of shot,
I can see the spring mud on them,
weighing him down as he marches along.

## Bike Ride

We are all of us
reeling up the hill
and into the wind.
The little one is perched
behind you on the carryseat,
gliding his wings,
rocking the back wheel.
And we three are pedalling
hard in your wake.
The girls stand up
and jerk, jerk, coast
through the puddles
making slurry water skirt
straight up over our feet,
but we don't care.
We are laughing and puffing
under our own steam.
It's the first warm day
before spring really comes,
so we are feeling lucky to be alive,
just riding along.
And it suddenly comes to me
how I used to dream
simply of this.

# Jenny Morris

## Visitation

A weighty flutter overhead.
An owl comes out of the night
moves through darkness to settle.
Donna La Morte whirrs down trailing
feathers like shroud garments.
Turns, her beak becomes fleshy lips.
She speaks lies in a language
I don't want to understand.
She holds up a mask to hide her skull.
A stiff white Venetian face,
almond spaces curved in gold.
Black holes in her head. She is all
brocade, lace, gauze, sequins
and false silver flowers.
She is all Carnival, insincere.
I attack her in silence.

## Painted Woman

This silver platter's heavy
with John's head in a pool
of dark blood which stains
his beard, drips over the lip.
I have to hold it away from my skirt.

Dish-dead he looks me in the eye
as if he understands. More than
my erect stepfather with his smirk
and confused smoke-white hair.
Under her hood Herodias
takes stock, she won't lose her head.
Vicious, nagging old bitch.
Perhaps now she'll be satisfied.
Finally I've done the right thing.
Pleasing the old man is essential
for a girl in my position.
Flames light up my night
as I shimmer in my Venetian red dress.
We're all shades of scarlet here.
That stupid dancing's hateful,
moving my hips, uncovering myself.
Pour more wine for heaven's sake.

# Jonathan Morton

### Prague i

Sitting there
in that dark courtyard
I watched the starlight break
across your forehead
spreading and fading in the folds of your hair

You said we were like two pigeons
huddled up close
trying to keep warm

I wanted to take your hand, then
and kiss you
to bring you into me
but you never looked up

Your mind stayed focused on holding the moment
and imprinting it for ever
in my brain

### Budapest i

The sight of that old man
made me take you off the road
into the park

It was evening
a brief lull in the thunderstorm
air thick and focused

The clearing was like some distorted golf course
all grass bunkers, curves and traps

The feel of mud on my hands and knees
the sound of your breath

I could hear people walking
on the other side of the trees

I didn't notice till we got back
just how dirty we were

## Budapest ii

I remember once as we lay naked in a hotel room, my arm draped
sleepily across your breast, the soft warmth of your lips brushing
against my neck as you slept. I could hear the traffic drifting
gently past the window and the sound of people talking as they
went to work. I watched the sun quietly part the blinds and creep
into the room, glittering on the sweat that still hung on our
bodies. I moved my hand down your side, you stirred in your
sleep, a smile flickering across your face. I closed my eyes and
tried to rest. I could still taste you on my lips as I slipped into
unconsciousness, sweet and salty.

Why can I only reach you in images?

## Prague ii

Back at the island hostel
I can't stop thinking about Wednesday
about leaving.

You surprise me with a trip to a nearby castle
where we hitch a ride round with
a German tour group
Once inside you take my hand and
run through a roped off doorway
into the ruined garden where
weeds and rose bushes slip gently
over stone
over me
looking up at your face
your eyes closed
mouth open
drinking in the air and sweat and scent

Back at the island hostel
I can't stop thinking about Wednesday
about leaving.

## Brussels

Here, once more at the border of Europe
I try and shut you from my mind
I try and cut the lovers' bind
it's the only way that I can cope

I push down memories as fast as I can
your voice screaming through the square
I just pretend I do not care
that I caught and held you when you ran

to me, crying, begging me not to leave
I remember your weight in my arms
the pain at being the one who harms
you, the one to push you down, to cleave

our private world. But I find once more
the plastic station pulls me back
keeps me moving on the right track
Its restriction is still the only cure.

# Kate North

---

## So You're Welsh Are You?

*Do you speak it?*
                No
*Were you born in . . .*
                No
*Do you like rugby?*
                Well,
if you mean can I kick,
                yes.

This is on the left,
to the right I feel the other edge.
These people from where I am
are ploughing their soil until it's just a pile of sand.
I want to speak to them, say
you only have the right to feed so much.

Once a girl told me,
*I'm not a freak show you know,*
*if you want to hear something Welsh watch S4C.*
I'm tired of its crippling tones,
how about watching me.

Sometimes after Brains,*
her mouth grew legs,
running away it betrayed her head.

She was all *Gwlad, gwlad*
*Llanfarpwllgwyngyllgogerychwyndrobwyll*Ican'truddywellsayit.
Then I found I was stuck in a corner shouting about Arthur,
defending my King who is only a myth.

*\* Alcoholic drink brewed in Cardiff*

## Written for the Only Woman

The only woman that I have always known,
she loves me like this.

She kept me in a fortress,
no, a tower.
I had long blond hair,
I had a big white horse, of course.

She dined me like a queen every night,
on quince and toast;
my only maid ladling my milk into champagne flutes,
then I'd sprinkle chocolate drops on the top.

Now I'm gnawing at my limbs,
something that I can't stop.

The only woman
what does she see?
A girl who can't stop because she tastes so good.

## Testament

### 1

This is twelve years ago
waiting on my bed with my back to the door,
the corkboard I stare at is like marble
veins then an underground map,
it's a riverbed deposit.

The nearing thump,
thump, thump,
of my mother's footstep precedes the parting of her lips.

I've got the screenplay in my brain
as we fly through the tornado
clicking our shoes.
When my mother lands she throws over my bookcase onto the
floor.

### 2

Ten minutes have passed
so I start the salvage operation,
searching for breakages with Mr Sheen
hovering in her Sunday space.

Today and other scary times
I find a book in a box under my bed.
A family book of purple and gold,
I feel like I've never seen it before.
Edging back the cover I block away
sounds of slamming cutlery drawers downstairs.

While she folds serviettes
I smooth down illustrated pages.
Men around a table,
a man with a lamb as a yoke,
old men with long hair,
women at wells and with pottery.

The cover is made of oil
so it plays the slippery fish in my hands.
I place it back in the box
and go down to eat.

# Helen Oswald

## Second Language

I am wondering if this shyness is yours,
or only belongs in your second language,
English. It is absent from your third –
your eyes and hands are fluent, expert
gestures searching in the air
for something you cannot see,
but know is there.

Acting hostess, I am keeping you at bay
with, 'How long have you been here?' And,
'What have you seen so far?' 'You,' you say,
'I have seen you.' I laugh, startled.
You smile, pleased to have caused
shock in another tongue,
and your careful fingers seem to tie a knot.

## Thread

A single gold thread trapped in the weave of this old, blue
                                                  table-cloth
catches the light and our imaginations like a comet and we
                                                       guess
where it hails from. You set the scene: a rickety loom,
                                          a sweatshop
in Bahrain, a sari fraying at the seam, arrival in cold English
                                                  rooms.

No. I say. It's January in Tennessee. A Christmas tree lashed to
                                                    the rack,
tinsel blows off into fields, snags on a soft-skulled cotton bud.
It's picked and packed and spun up East, where bashful Jimmy
                                                    Stewart
handles quality control, dreams of a blond-haired girl, and lets
                                                    slip.

We're on a roll. It's not a thread, but a flaxen skein off
                                                    Marilyn's head
that caught the sleeve of JFK as they hit the gas out past New
                                                    Jersey.
Next day, a factory inspection, a golden handshake with the
                                                    chairman,
he promises a secretary the moon, the hair trails off; the rest is
                                                    mystery.

But as we speak you pick at it and finally you tease it out,
twirl it between your finger and thumb, a spinner,
but the magic's gone. The night is dark. We turn the television on.


## Easter Parade

That year it made a change from cowboys and Indians
and the hyena yelping of my brother as he performed
another ritual scalping on my unrelenting head.

We knew about the thrill of blood and so *The Passion*
offered brute drama brought with deep conviction
to the well spattered stage of our back garden.

My brother sawed up stakes in Mum's new greenhouse,
recasting them from former roles piercing the hearts
of midnight vampires, to nail three crosses.

I tore worn bed-sheets into strips of loin cloth,
anointed the feet of a bear with Pears shampoo
and left it overnight in a geranium Gethsemane.

Good Friday came. A green road to Calvary,
rude wooden trucks transported toy disciples, solemn
through the grassy streets of our Jerusalem.

Our parents, Pontius Pilates, stood watching
from an upstairs window, horrified and yet
unable to wash their hands of it.

Beyond the hedge a mound of earth prepared
beneath the holly tree that had supplied
a crown of thorns. Two gollies, thieves, awaited Christ,

and me and my brother, stretched to an unruly crowd,
having a good stab at it, yelling: 'Crucify him! Crucify him!'
Two small gods making it all happen.

## One Over

Stiff faces spill from cars into silence,
herd up the churchyard, shy away like sheep.
The same crowd looks immaculate, but tense,
that danced right through the night and fell asleep
under the marquee at Jacko's wedding
last May. We blew across the lawn – bright
crumpled litter – and drove home laughing.
Now we are all too awake but chalk white,
standing beside the hole we want to shun.
Suddenly you're there in my dry mind's eye,
raising your sparkling glass – a wry oration,
wishing the newly-weds good luck, goodbye.
The mute grave catches my breath, mouth open
wide to welcome the tongue of your spoken
life.

## Seas

Long after you have gone, seagulls
are upwardly mobile outside my window,
calling in the singular language of their trade.
Their sharp eyes interrogate the home brew
and pewter of an English sea. Way below,
the fretful summer traffic works itself up
like a red-faced, angry baby on the front.

The old pier has burnt itself out and rests,
intricate and empty as a dead bird's skeleton.
Water jostles light as if it's coming to the boil.
Far off a trawler fathoms out fish, its nets
work up a thirst for other seas beyond.
But sea is like that; too big to take in,
and not quite infinite enough.

# Helen Phillippo

## millers

They come in
look around
stand at the counter
like Easter Island rocks
order
food and a cup of tea
chips and eggs a slice of bread.
They collect their mugs
put teaspoons inside
eager to stir,
moving over to a chosen table
like steam trains
with their hot drinks.
They put them down
they put their bags
on adjacent seats
they might take off
a hat or a coat
lying it on the table
next to their mugs.
They sit down
get comfortable
maybe light up a
cigarette
taking quick, sharp drags
staring directly in front –
whatever's happening –

these people aren't shy.
Here comes the food
stub out that cigarette,
a gift of
knife and fork and napkin
nothing to confuse
straightforward and honest
just like the food.
Chew chew
chewing silently
unblinkingly ahead
pausing for slurps of tea
repeating and repeating,
now tongues searching and
probing round teeth.
Then finishing, gathering up
coats and bags and hats
walking straight out the
door,
leaving the debris of
half-eaten chips and
spreading yellow eggs.
For some
this is not
a novelty.

## information

Teaspoons in a mug
pressed up hard and cold
like all of us in here.
They're the only things that match –
the teaspoons –
everything else is odd
especially the customers,
people of indiscriminate age

dressed in old clothes
cheap clothes
dirty clothes
clothes that hang and hang.
Just watching,
people at the counter
any food brought out or
drinks taken away
someone going to the toilet.
They don't look in envy
or hatred or confusion,
they just look, just watch.
But
maybe I've misjudged them
they could be gathering information
for a book or a screenplay
about all the people like me
who come in, buy tea
and stare at them silently,
scribbling the occasional note.

## the meeting

In the front corner of the café
opposite the window
overlooking the alleyway
and adjacent to the door
through which come blasts of
even colder, icier air
than is already circulating around us
as the customers enter and leave,
under medieval depictions of saints
and poppies next to the sea
sit two men on a table for four.
The older one, probably in his fifties,

is wearing the same
blue jeans that he's worn for months
or longer
and a big woolly jumper, this one
dark green – he has others
of different colours and degrees of brightness.
He pulls his fingers
through his coarse grey hair
which has fallen out, monk-like, on top
moving his fringe from around his eyes as
he talks to the man opposite
who has deep lines around his
mouth, his cheeks,
short dark hair
and a Roman nose.
He's talking about printing presses
and pot-bellied stoves
as he pulls at the fleshy lobe of his ear.
The older man goes on to say
that his fingertips are now permanently
numb, that he can't feel the money
in his pocket and drops things
because he can't judge how hard
he's gripping them;
people look at him as though he's stupid
or mad
as objects fall to the floor
around him.
His hands are greasy
smelling of metal
– the taste of blood –
his dirty fingernails
on thick blunt digits
bitten to the extreme.
Both slurp at cups of tea,
the dark-haired man
rolls the odd cigarette and tries

to smoke secretly, almost guiltily,
He's making a rocket out of
coke cans and paper clips
fuelled by air and water,
it's gonna be a great achievement
he says.

## cold, sick and tired

I've been in here too long
I can no longer focus
in this weak yellow light
which filters down through random
yellow plastic squares
lazily,
like it can't be bothered.
I feel cold next to the door
but I'd feel just as cold
around the corner
there's no difference –
no source of heat to aim for.
I feel a bit sick
watching her in her
baby blue jumper and
wrinkled grey skin
like the clingfilm which
covers the cakes –
pliable and weak.
I'm sick of seeing that
tub of hot chocolate
sitting above the microwave
that never gets used
and the boxes of Jaffa
cakes and Mars bars
anticipating their expiry dates.
I've been in here too long.

# Sibyl Ruth

## Cyclops

When they lifted it up and away from me
they didn't say 'What a lovely girl.' Or boy.
They took my baby and examined it on a metal trolley.
Hurried phone calls were made.
After that was like falling down a swirling tunnel.
A blur. Strange colours. I can't remember.

Once, in the middle of the night, when I couldn't sleep
with the bump being so uncomfortable, I do remember thinking,
suppose there's something wrong with it?

I know now they are not going to wheel my bed back to ward 6.
Instead I will be given a side room,
away from the chat of the women who were my neighbours,
them and their normal babies.
I will be offered counselling,
given details of the appropriate organisations.

It goes on breathing in a plastic box.
So white and old looking. Like it's travelled a great way.
It isn't exactly a face.
Not with those added bits, those openings.
I thought at first there might be some sort of operation.

It could be something I've done.
Perhaps I went over the limit for alcohol.
Ate peanuts. Or pâté. Or modified tomatoes.

Something, anything past the sell by date.
I tried to be careful.
But these days you can't be sure what's safe.

In time my baby will become a curiosity,
a specimen in a collection,
an example with a Latin name.
People who were my friends will say 'Never mind.
You can always try again.'

For one second I was happy.
After the long hours of struggling and yelling,
of slurping gas and air.
Labour over. A battle won.

Relations are coming.
It was too late to stop them.
They'll not want to look in the cot.
But they won't be able to help themselves.
They won't say 'Congratulations' but 'How are you coping?'
They will not offer me cards and balloons.
And the flowers round my bed will be like a funeral.

## Full House

Surrounded by stubborn furniture,
all yours.

Double-sided bookcases,
stacks of little tables.
Oak cabinets, sideboards, cupboards.
The uncomfortable chaise longue,
an out-of-tune piano.

Pieces glower from every corner.
Obstructing windows,
they cast odd shadows,
darken doorways.

There's plenty of room, you say.
I could make the occasional gesture with a duster.
Be more accommodating.

While they graze my shins for fun
snag sleeves, tweak fingernails,
nip my vulnerable toes.
And they won't be moved.

I'd imagined owning less.
Somewhere unvarnished, uninsured –
bare walls and floors,
with wind chimes, maybe lanterns.
Stars looking down on a shared emptiness.

## The Wrong Verb

This room is a hot country.
Our hands become frantic
making tracks, marks over sheets.
They find tangents, complications.

We're so quiet it hurts.
Bare elbows pressed on the grain of the table.
The creak and shift of rickety chairs
*It's work* we'll say, if anyone asks.

\*

Hurricanes don't visit the town I'm from.
But there was a small tornado last week, quite near
which lifted somebody's roof right off.
The story got into all the papers.

*

Now I may never get to utter
the words *This is madness*
*No good will come of this . . .*
or scrawl an urgent *P.S. Burn this letter*.

*

After peanuts and beer
the train rocks us back through the hot green evening.
We talk a lot about children –
how brilliant, how exhausting they are.
Once or twice we refer to partners.

At New Street, we separate.
I aim a kiss at your face –
the scratch of new mown grass.
And brush your hand,
that warm, curled animal.

It will take both of us some time
to come home.

# Rhian Saadat

## Red Dress

*C'était une robe étonnante*

is usually how the story begins,
yard after yard of
red silk
fanning its wings over a
neon-stripped world
like some exotic moth freed
from its forty-watt circus ring.

*Mais, la belle?*

Priceless.
They assured the crowd
Mlle Fossagrives was
firmly bound to the top of the tower,
absolutely zero risk involved in
the wearing of this piece,
a genuine Lelong meant
comprehensive insurance
paid for by *Vogue*.

Most of us, earth bound
in our low voltage macs,
knew it was for real.

It was the way she fluttered out
into the sky, holding the rail
like an ice-cream cone – hey yup,
strawberry from Berthillon.
A shade that matched the shoes.

When it happened – no,
she didn't fall, she didn't slip,
simply spiralled upwind,
leaving the crew in a flat spin about
dying film and exposed light,
so that, no one got the one shot

*étonnante*

of the naked creature in fruity shoes
and red silk parachute.

## Waiting for News of Mehdi

I found your radio this morning
signalling from under the pillow
its steady interference
itching the skin.

You've been wearing it all night
these last few years, locked
close to your cheek – the signal
wakes you on the hour – news

from Tehran, prayers and songs,
arabesques, escaping on waves –
beautiful voices in measured tones
imprisoned in black, their intonations

linking your blood to home, and to
somewhere beyond, the tiny room
holding your brother – silent, save
the signals he sends you, cell
to cell.

## Offerings

You always brought pomegranates
in suitcases,
not the small, supermarket kind;
vast orange baubles radiating a
natural heat.
You encouraged us to eat like
savages,
the pink of our mouths hitting the
combined juices of bulging seeds,
laughing at impossibilities,

talking of purifying blood.
Your excess baggage would ease
across the sitting-room floor; carpets,
so densely knotted they folded into
thin air; saffron hats
embroidered with poems,
strings of pistachio nuts,
an old telescope, a Persian astrolabe.
A paradise garden on a miniature scale.

All this. And tales.
We draw close for the latest one; time lost
in a Tehran jail. Head Gardener,
you smile, fainter now.
I grew pomegranates, gathered dates.
Of a different kind.

Cutting the flesh from another fruit,
your shirt-sleeve rolled,
we read the scars –
begin to understand why your
hands tremble
without something to hold.

# Owen Sheers

## Deaf and Dumb

I know I shouldn't have stared,
empty as the carriage was, just the three of us
riding the last tube home.

But your shared absence was a sound impossible to ignore,
as were your magician's hands, performing word tricks –
now you see them, now you don't –

accompanied by your mis-dubbed mouths,
actors caught in a foreign film, lip-reading from
a different script to the subtitles of your fingers.

And your faces – expressions of the silent movie star,
eyebrow active, drama masks falling from smile to tear,
wide eyes, open and honest. Rare.

At times you laughed and there was love in her eye I swear,
and I'm sure I saw her hand flutter over her heart
more than once, and I thought I understood.

But how could I? Dumb opposite you,
just my dark concave reflection in the plastic window
and the tunnel wind in my ear,

and my hands, my clumsy, inarticulate hands in my lap
as I sat there, watching you,
deaf to your stories and your long, loud language of silence.

## Breaking Hearts

There is only the blunt aggression of the sledge-hammer,
and the tearing of wood. These are the rules.

Stubborn in its solidness,
frayed at its head, where a thousand blows
have sunk its bite deep into tree flesh,

the wedge is gripped by this, which it is driving apart –
like a lover, who holds tight to the one who is leaving,
the one who is breaking their heart.

Another hit and I have broken its centre,
the Gordian knot of whirlpool wood,
the embryo curled in its womb.

Another, and a leaf of bark breaks free, its underside etched
with the circuit-board work of woodworm,
the wiring of the grain.

A final swing and the log gives,
breaks with a sigh, lets go and leans –
the broken heart of a tree, an iron tooth, lying in between.

## The Year in Four Haikus

    Spring
Swallows crotchet and
minim the telephone wires;
sing in crossed lines.

    Summer
Bees go down at the
lips of foxgloves, nervous like
a lover's first time.

Autumn
A spider has danced
a fingerprint in the space
between two branches.

Winter
Nests are bloodclots in
the veins of the tree; the rooks
a passing infection.

## Life Class

It was the only time I ever saw him still;
in Art, crouched and serious over a page,
his bitten pencil working quickly,
pulling a sketch from the paper.

He was good, but never got the chance to carry on,
not after that fight, when his flick and slit
got him sent away, cuffed and collared,
frog-marched through the gates of Cardiff Nick.

Although, from what I heard, he carried on creating;
tipping a pan of hissing water over a snitch,
painting him in blisters and splashes of burns.
A life drawing, stained by a skin graft –

the surgeon's signature to his work of art.

# Oliver Shelley

## Milk

In the corner sat a dairy man,
his blond hair held up in a chip bag
and his white surgeon's gown
flecked by the slop of churning.

When he came in he had ambled,
shuffling in his gum boots
and looking weighed down,
as if milk had caught in each one.

He worked his way past my table
and in the easy roll of the haunches
that stood out in the tail of his coat
and in the swing of his hips as he sat

I saw how he was a cowboy:
a man so immersed in milk
that he had bettered Cleopatra
and had it running in his blood.

His forearms were as pale as veal
and, peeling off two latex gloves,
each finger came out like a Dairy Pop,
the nails as clear as gelatine.

But his silence was the most cow-like;
how he sat in his bulk and waited,
only shifting in his chair to gaze about
with a quiet bred from bewilderment.

Then his plate came and he set to,
almost giddy as he cut up the meat.
He worked through each forkful
with a rancher's greed, only pausing

to squeeze ketchup from a plastic tomato
which, as he held it there in his fist,
looked like a miniature udder,
the stalk changed into a teat.

## Dummy

That granite man in Bratislava
with a head like a compressed truck
and a neck strung tight as a pylon
who spun his glass on the table,
this way and then that, brooding,
furious; each look he sent our way
so impassive and blunt
that cruelty was simplified.

Until his wife and baby came
and delight unwrapped him
so that he took the child
and shook it till its laughter frothed
then putting its dummy in his mouth
he sucked it like a cartoon calf.
And all the while his wife sat back
and bit the quick from her nails.

## Young woman from Höchstenbach

My cousin's footsteps under the window,
the door opening and any warmth lost.
It is still night and the curtains
are flat with the cold of it,
every angle in the house is sharp.
Downstairs the hall clock chimes
too clearly for any sleep
and soon he will feed the stove:
that one wail of the iron door
draws us from our beds to dress
in clothes we wear all week.
There's no comfort in these days;
we wash cold and eat bread
then follow the rest to the fields:
I throw seed from a leather bag
that used to hold my books.

# Kris Siefken

## Covey's Landing, Georgia

I sit,
only inches above the water,
the dry crumbling timbers of the decayed jetty
fossilised history beneath my re-crossing legs.

Somewhere upstream, around the reach\*,
a spaniel jumps into the water,
the sound carried on the current
like a child's leaf and twig boat.

The sun slips,
casting a deep purple shadow
from the willow on the opposite bank:
those boughs under which I snatched my third childhood kiss.
The willow's cold, inverted twin greets me:
eager grey hands caressing my thighs:
evening seeks refuge amidst a forest of hair.

\*

The shadow spreads. Time transgresses.
*August 1842*,
and the spaniel's doggy paddle
becomes a man's frantic breaststroke:
Nathaniel Covey swimming for his life.

Behind him, amongst the trees, hounds complain,
torn by the same thorns that tore their master's quarry.

Voices roll through the heavy air:
angry men promise violence and chains.

Suddenly,
shots crackle in the darkness,
like moths popping in a candle's open flame.

Off to my right another flash of light:
the orange bark of a gun's retort.

\*

All is quiet now,
even the stars have neglected the chase.

Slowly, mid-stream, a deeper shadow appears,
kicking softly for shore.
Moonlight snakes in the water behind it.

I lean forwards to touch it,
brush wet hair and then it is gone:

just another shadow lurking in the waters beneath me.

\* *A bend in a river*

## Travelling Backwaters

The canoe's bow parts water
like warm butter
caving under the heavy silver knives of my grandmother's
house.

Back then my legs dangled
and eight-year-old eyes met tabletop food as an equal:
eyeball to buttered corn eyeball.
Now
those same legs fill a canoe's open body
like timber:
two flawed, felled journeyman logs
floating in a Missouri creek.

The melted river slaps
at the polished plywood sides,
rippling against them like cuckoo wings in flight.

Blond, sunshine curls
trail the boat's wake:
a high-school prom queen drowned in the water,
oblivious
to the mosquitoes dancing above.

# Maggie Simmons

## Too Much to Ask?

I'd like to know that
if I were to swallow something evil
you'd stick your fingers down my throat.
But then again, perhaps you'd let me struggle
and watch as I squirm and wriggle?

If I'd made that trade with a sanguine hand
would you snatch me from His wintry
grasp, lift me from the spiral of His wrath
or abandon me to the quicksand,
and thrill to the chill of it all?

Would my blackened heart prove too slippery
to grip, to hold and fit inside your velvet case?
Would it stain the plush whilst filling the space
with a blood too dark and thick
for even you to savour?

## A Friend

'It was hell but it was worth it,'
she confessed in club-loud whispers.

I clutched my breath and waited for more.

A stream of torrid gossip coursed
steadily out from those pneumatic lips.

I nodded conspiratorially.

The oohs and aahs of abandoned vowels
landed with a clatter on the tiled floor.

I bit the rim of my glass

as she spilled the unsavoury beans
lavishly across the polished bar.

I offered a cigarette

she snatched a light from a passing
stranger firing yet another touch-paper.

I blinked in awe.

My eyes opened too late. I'd been left
heavy with the weight of her confidences.

# Barbara Watts

## Now That's My Kind of Oasis

Yesterday I saw a yellow A-frame tent on the beach
Canute and Midas were camped out inside
singing, brawling, with talks of canoeing
playing Snap, unafraid of the tide

Guys, are you crazy? –
my voice so loud I shook the shells
but in the end it just bounced off a gull
so what the hell

The guide rope – neat and purposeful
had the makings of a prow
and old Canute, his arms were oars
if ever I saw oar arms
whereas Midas could drop anchor with a glance
the brush of one fat finger.

On the first night smugly bunking down
we drank whatever came to hand:
we drank sand.

The boys were rocks,

the tide line didn't scare us –
lucky splash, we came in on the tide,
we had our mouths open, our watches on
turn-ups were unrolled

and all of us sharing one soul like a dingy, begrudgingly
and the sound of somebody humming *The Owl and the Pussy Cat*
and me thinking how I could tip out the sea water with the
empty bean cans
and them planning on filling the bean cans with sand
as some sort of barricade.


## I Found My Man in a Snow-Shaker

Arctic Parka, bins,* cold winds blowing
and he's yours;
ice-cool eyes, whipped 'tache, chapped lip
just a constellation short . . .

    He's yours and only yours

Warm hood like hands upon his head
as sure as Mother's paw;
icicles hang from his brow
warn about the thaw . . .

    He's cautious and he's yours

Pockets packed with Kendal Mint Cake
swaggers from the snowy blast
produces seven bright red roses
salutes like they're a flag, half-mast . . .

    Commits with like to last

A creek of frost, the perfect host
opens wide his hamper lid,
snaps the blanket as he lays it
says, 'at least we both have bibs' . . .

Survivalist ad-lib

What's a holiday without marmalade
bread that's freshly thawed?
The rubber rim that keeps him trim
in time, will keep him warm . . .

Introducing himself in a storm

Swollen eyelids guide his eyeballs
like the compass on the ship;
whiteness even in the darkness
hasn't had a wink of kip . . .

Mouth stung shut like a zip

* *Short for binoculars*

# Sara Wingate-Gray

## To You Who Speak No English

First contact
is not a name, a face
or words of indefinite introduction
but our laugh at the way my toes curl up
and over, your five, light brown stubs.
I know it is time to eat not when you say
'Let's have lunch' or 'Dinner's ready' but when
fingers splayed, stretching as if to catch every imaginary grain
                                                    of rice
(for as my mother told me there are millions starving in China)
your right hand flutters in front of your mouth like a twirling fan.
You teach me how to write my name
all over again, and how to sleep three on a wooden pallet
net curtains and clothes pegs our only arms against the
                                        nocturnal swarms.
Beancurd milk and cake at breakfast and you sit and braid
                                            my hair
fingers crumbed with sponge and thick white icing
I spend the day picking dandruff-sized droplets from blond
                                            tangles
whose strands you steal from a hairbrush to show to your friends.

Our silence on the outside
is punctuated by slaps
as mosquitoes dance across our skin.
And to you who speak no English
words are barriers.

Because, I, who speak no Chinese,
must let them fall blankly on the ground.
Instead, I just sit and think and laugh
and know it was simply enough
the way my toes
curled up
and over
your five, light brown stubs.

## I Played the Beat of Love Upon Your Belly

I play the beat of love upon your belly
watch my fingers as they skip across your skin.
One time two time rag time bath time
tips slapping rhythmically down like tap water
which has left you with bristles of silk
smoothed like a waxed violinist's bow.
Sonorous, the beat expounds,
I tap harder on your rib
hope that the hollow echo will reveal
a secret trap-door to your insides
where cadences weighed in cups like sugar
flutter between your rib-caged keys.
So, this is love.
A pounding remonstrative surge
which goads me to run my fingers
through your knotty, wet hair.
I played the beat of love upon your belly
and I ran out of notes.

# Morgan Yasbincek

## perth

all of a sudden
you were owned 'my city'
blue as a fairy wren
as the neon pulse of heat
the arc of an atmosphere

i was different
because i was from
a west coast city
of concrete grey soils
where the native trees
sprout brilliant hairy flowers
and black parrots shout down rain
with flaked pine cones

i wanted to say you in a sentence
to catch the sweet musty smell of soil
exposed to heating sky
and offer it to someone
who would have to imagine
what i mean

## magpie

at 3 a.m. the cat wakes me
the house has inhaled this heat
smoke, eucalypt thick
from circling bushfires
rings the city

sirens bellow and sigh

a magpie sticks the scissors
of its beak into the smoky sky and sings
this complexity

an ominous coherence
a scattering sound
describes itself

the scissors of its beak catch
falling saliva in my throat
pincers the bones of my sternum

runnels of sound
ease their slow burn through
first skin, second skin

preclude a blue city

## reallycrap

used to the catch of the 'y'
like a dragnet

the hard vowel almost
overshoots the plosive
in a comic plummet

a cat falling off the wardrobe
her forelegs raised
like a human in a hold-up


## out toward anglesey

justice meditates on her view of the strait
centuries scoot past and muddle like oyster catchers
the T of her clavicle is set steady, her gaze
turned down to her heart

she calculates –
her biceps build with the weight
in the scales, muscle deepening down
through bone, through catacomb to streams

she's listening
to the chatter of generations
one for each wave, each sigh

under her garment, which is loose
and holds its fashion against time
the beating centre clears its rhythm
and begins to whisper back the course:

the black dragon, penned in
by welsh mountains blows steam
over snowdonia

a baby is exposed in a castle

a miner dies of tb aged thirty-five

his son remembers red stuff after the cough

justice has the sword across her knee
the balance of the unused blade
is easily mistaken for an emblem
its tilt could slip it from her gown

she needs her quiet, her solitude
she may act yet
or erode in the icy coastal blast
before the fold comes down
and the seagull floats off her helmet

# Notes on Contributors

**Paul Batchelor** was born in Newcastle. Has never won a poetry competition, been on a shopping spree, precipitated the apocalypse, but he has bought the wrong ticket, caught the wrong train. He works as a cleaner, but doesn't consider it a career. Writes a poem every morning. Doesn't consider that a career either.

**Lawrence Bradby** started reading poetry in his twenties, during a long period of illness. 'As it dragged on for month after month, people would ask me what it was like. I started memorising bits of poems – angry, sardonic, evasive – anything to put a bit of fizz into those conversations about my health. It's stuck with me since then.'

**Sue Butler** grew up in Hertfordshire and since then has worked and travelled in Germany, Russia, Uzbekistan, China and Sri Lanka. She now lives in Norfolk.

**Sarah Corbett**'s first collection of poems, *The Red Wardrobe* (Seren, 1998) was shortlisted for a Forward Prize and the T. S. Eliot Prize. She received an Eric Gregory Award in 1997 and an MA in Creative Writing from UEA in 1998. She currently lives in Yorkshire with her husband and baby son where she is writing a second collection of poems and a film script.

**Polly Clark** was born in Toronto and brought up in Lancashire and the Borders. She has pursued several careers including zookeeping in Edinburgh and teaching English in Hungary. She won an Eric Gregory Award in 1997 and her first collection *Kiss* (Bloodaxe, 2000) is a Poetry Book Society Recommendation.

**Rachel Crookes** was born in the Midlands in 1979. She has just finished her degree at the University of East Anglia. She is now living in Norwich, practising decadence.

**David Evans** was born in Cardiff in 1969. He is a postgraduate student at Norwich School of Art and Design.

**Ivy Garlitz** was born in Miami. She was recently awarded a Ph.D. in Creative and Critical Writing at the University of East Anglia. Her poems have appeared in *The Honest Ulsterman*, *Poetry Review*, *Rialto*, *Smith's Knoll* and *Thumbscrew*. Her poem 'The Writer's Beginning' won the *Woman's Hour* sonnet competition. Her first pamplet, *A Better Life*, is published by the Bay Press. She currently lives in Suffolk with her husband.

**Anna Garry** teaches Creative Writing at the University of East Anglia. At Manchester University she studied Biology and completed a Ph.D. in Political Science. A graduate of the MA in Creative Writing at UEA, she has been published in *Critical Quarterly*, and has recently completed a novel. She edited *Lava*, a short story collection in the UEA <text> series.

**Helen Goddard** was born in Northampton in 1975. She grew up in Poole, going on to study French and Linguistics at Magdalen College, Oxford. Her wide range of interests includes art, astrology, theatre and psychology. Her current poems reflect her fascination for the quirks of human consciousness.

**Karen Goodwin** has recently won the Eric Gregory Award for poets under thirty. She was born in Swansea in 1976 and studied for her first degree at Aberystwyth University. Her poems have been published in *Poetry Wales*, *Stand* and *Oxygen* – a Seren anthology of new Welsh poets. Her first collection has the working title *Song Lines*.

**Eleanor Green** was born in Cambridge in 1978. She is studying English Literature and Drama at the University of East Anglia.

**Jane Griffiths** was born in Exeter, but brought up in Holland. She read English at Oxford, where her poem 'The House' won the Newdigate Prize and where she is now completing a doctorate on the Tudor poet John Skelton. She won an Eric Gregory Award in 1996, and her first collection of poems, *A Grip on Thin Air*, is published by Bloodaxe.

**Ramona Herdman** was born in London. Raised in transit. Published in *Staple*, *Ikon*, and various titles in the UEA <text> series. Lives in Norwich. Dances immoderately. Tells inadvisably. Currently in debt.

**Andrea C Holland** was born in London but spent fourteen years studying and teaching in the United States before returning to the UK in 1995. She has an MA in Creative Writing (University of Massachusetts) and now teaches writing at the Norwich School of Art and Design, and American Studies at UEA. She has several poetry and non-fiction publications in the UK and US, including *Rialto*, *Other Poetry* and *Phoebe*.

**Matthew Hollis** was born in Norwich in 1971, studied at Edinburgh, and works as an editor at the Oxford University Press. He won an Eric Gregory Award in 1999, third prize in the National Poetry Competition, 1996, and his pamphlet *The Boy on the Edge of Happiness* (Smith/Doorstop, 1996) was a prize winner in the 1995 Poetry Business Competition. He is co-editor of *Strong Words: Modern Poets on Modern Poetry* (Bloodaxe, 2000).

**Helen Ivory** was born in Bedfordshire in 1969. She received a BA (hons) in Cultural Studies at Norwich Art School in 1998 and in 1999 won an Eric Gregory Award. She has published poems in *Ambit* and *Orbis* and currently lives in Norfolk where she is working on her first collection.

**David Allen Lambert** was born in 1967 in Dayton, Ohio. He wrote his first real poem on the eve of his seventeenth birthday and has not stopped since. David came to the UK in 1988. He has worked and performed with various creative writing groups, and reads frequently in the local area. Previous published poetry has appeared in TVP *Savouries*, *Birdsuit* and *White Noise*.

**Sarah Law** was born in Norwich, studied English at Cambridge and completed a Ph.D. on the influence of mysticism on modernist women writers at Queen Mary and Westfield College in 1997. Since returning to Norwich she has concentrated on writing poetry; her full-length collection, *Bliss Tangle*, was published by Stride in 1999.

**Julia Lee** was born in 1978. She took a degree in English and American Literature at Warwick University and is now on the Creative Writing MA at the University of East Anglia. She lives in Twickenham.

**Joanne Limburg** grew up in London and now lives in Cambridge. She won an Eric Gregory Award in 1998 and her first book *Feminismo* is published by Bloodaxe, September 2000.

**John McCullough** was born in Watford in 1978. He studied English and Creative Writing at the University of East Anglia and is currently at the University of Sussex taking an MA in Sexual Dissidence. His work has appeared in numerous magazines and anthologies including the *Sex* and *writing on drugs* titles in the UEA <text> series.

**Andrew McDonnell** was born in 1977, grew up in Shoreham Village, Kent, before going on to study for a BA (hons) in Cultural Studies at Norwich School of Art and Design. He lives in Norwich and can be contacted at quickspace99@hotmail.com

**Lee McNicoll** writes: 'Since I was able to hold a pen I've been writing poems, stringing words together to evoke some kind of emotion, and this has continued into my English Literature degree. I hope to branch out into children's literature, and to ensure that every word out there finds its voice (they often have so much more to say than people).'

**Kona Macphee** was born in London in 1969 and grew up in Melbourne, Australia. In the late 1980s she studied musical composition at the Conservatorium of Sydney, violin at the University of Sydney and worked as an apprentice motorbike mechanic at an auto repair shop. She subsequently took degrees in Digital Systems and Computer Science at Monash University in Melbourne and completed an M.Sc. in Computer Science at Cambridge in 1999. She received an Eric Gregory Award in 1998.

**Mary Macrae Gibson** was born in Morocco into a diplomatic family and dragged up in wartime Britain by disapproving relatives. She began writing short stories and poetry after retirement from teaching and parenthood and is now also writing about her childhood. She lives in Norfolk with her partner, two lapcats and a laptop.

**Neil Martin** is twenty-one years old and has just completed a degree in English and American literature at UEA. He lives in Boston, Lincolnshire.

**Anika Moje** was born and raised in Berlin. She recently graduated from the University of East Anglia with a B.A. in Film and American Studies. Among her favourite things are dogs, mountains and Portland, Oregon.

**Jane Monson** was born in Slough and studied English and American Literature at UEA. Her degree included a year's study in Portland, Oregon where she started developing her poetry. Jane is now on the Creative Writing MA at UEA and is working towards a collection of her poems and photographs.

**Melissa Moore** lives with her husband and three children by the River Stour in Suffolk. She has been studying Creative Writing with the Centre for Continuing Education at UEA, and is now training to be a primary school teacher.

**Jenny Morris** has taught in this country and abroad. Her poetry and fiction have been published in numerous magazines and anthologies, and read on radio. She lives in Norwich.

**Jonathan Morton** was brought up in Berkshire and came to Norwich to study History with a minor in English Literature at the University of East Anglia. He is going on to take an MA.

**Kate North** is from Cardiff. She studied for her first degree at the University of Aberystwyth. She is currently completing an MA in Creative Writing at the University of East Anglia, while working on her first collection of poems and other prose projects. She is particularly interested in exploring issues of gender and religion.

**Helen Oswald** is a graduate of the Creative Writing MA at the University of East Anglia. Her poems have appeared in *Catapult*, an anthology of new writing, and in several magazines including *Rialto* and *Poetry London*. She received a commendation in the National Poetry Competition in 1999 and was a winner of the Blue Nose Competition in the same year. She was also shortlisted for the London Writers Award.

**Helen Phillippo** was born in Norwich, 1980. She is currently in the second year of a BA (hons) Cultural Studies degree at the Norwich School of Art and Design where she is specialising in, among other things, creative writing. Upon leaving she hopes to invent a time machine and travel back to the 1960s.

**Sibyl Ruth**'s collection *Nothing Personal* is published by Iron Press, 1995. She lives in Birmingham and during 1998/99 was the city's Poet Laureate. She teaches creative writing for the Open College of the Arts and at Birmingham University.

**Rhian Saadat** has been living in France since 1990 when she and her husband bought a restaurant in the Marches aux Puces. She teaches English and drama, and has written fiction and scripts for children. She is currently working on a first collection of poetry.

**Owen Sheers** was born in 1974. He was the winner of an Eric Gregory Award and the Vogue Young Writer's award in 1999. His first collection is *The Blue Book* (Seren, 2000).

**Oliver Shelley** was brought up in Oxfordshire and lives in Cambridge. He completed an MA in Creative Writing at the University of East Anglia in 1999. He is currently working on his first collection of poetry.

**Kris Siefken** was born in 1973 and graduated from UEA in 2000. He is currently a Creative Writing MA student at UEA. Kris would like to acknowledge his debt to Tim Seibles and David Corker whose enthusiasm for poetry helped Kris convince himself that 'poet' was a viable career option. His bank manager, however, would like to talk to both of them.

**Maggie Simmons** moved from London to north Norfolk in 1992, after a career as an art director in the music industry. Since then she has been a partner in a pub and restaurant business as well as studying for a BA in Film and English Studies at UEA. Although she has written many short stories and a screenplay, poetry is a relatively new passion.

**Barbara Watts** was born in Hereford and came to Norwich by car. She likes spiders, flicker books, making biscuits, writing poems and taking photos. Her poems are from an ongoing photo/poem/cut-out-and-keep project *Anything Can Be Addictive If You Really Put Your Mind To It*. For raffle tickets and further info contact babootoo@hotmail.com

**Sara Wingate-Gray** worked in Hong Kong in 1997 as a writer for the lifestyle magazine *'bc'*. She recently edited and designed *writing on drugs*, <text> 11 in the University of East Anglia's <text> series and has just graduated from UEA with a first class honours degree in English Literature and Creative Writing. She currently spends her time playing drums, freelancing for *Diva* magazine and body painting. She can be contacted via email at babybarb@x-magazine.co.uk

**Morgan Yasbincek** is a Western Australian writer. Her first collection of poetry, *Night Reversing*, won the 1997 Anne Elder Poetry Award and the 1997 Mary Gilmore Poetry Award. Her first novel *liv* has been published by Fremantle Arts Centre Press (http://facp.iinet.net.au). In 1998 she travelled to the UK where she completed a residency at the University of East Anglia. She teaches creative writing at Murdoch University, is developing her second collection of poetry and researching her Ph.D.

## The Litmus Test: Call for Submissions for *Reactions* 2001

Is your poetry acid or alkaline? As long as it isn't neutral, I'd like to hear from you . . .

The second edition of *Reactions* will appear in 2001. *Reactions* is a forum for new poetry by new poets. Submissions are therefore invited from writers who have had a first collection or pamphlet published (but not a second) and from those who have not yet reached that stage.

If you are interested in submitting work, please send five poems (no more or less) to me, Esther Morgan at The School of English and American Studies, University of East Anglia, Norwich NR4 7TJ.

The poems you send:

• can be on any subject, in any style and of any length.

• should be written in English, but can be in translation.
should be typed, with your name and address appearing

• clearly on each.

• must be your own original work.

• must not already be accepted for publication by any magazine (although poems which are due to appear in a first collection or anthology will be considered).

• should be accompanied by a covering letter which lists the titles of your poems, plus a short biography (of no more than 70 words).

• need to reach me by no later than March 31st 2001.

• must be good.

# PRETEXT

Subscribe to UEA's new International Literary Magazine Pretext and save 25% on the cover price. Published twice a year, Pretext aims to become one of the most exciting and innovative new literary magazines on the market.

Volume 2 will be published in October 2000, containing: interview with **Martin Amis**; poetry from **W. G. Sebald**; new fiction from **Peter Ho Davie**s, **Bridget O'Connor**, **Alan Beard**, **Jackie Gay**, and introducing bestselling Australian author **Andrew McGahan**, among many others. Subscription copies cost only £6 including p&p, instead of the rrp of £7.99 Send or email your name and address to:

**Julian Jackson,
Pretext Subscriptions,
English and American Studies,
University of East Anglia,
Norwich,
Norfolk,
NR4 7TJ
julian.jackson@uea.ac.uk**

Your copy will be mailed to you in September 2000, along with a direct debit form. Subscribers will also be included on our mailing list and be updated regularly on our publications.

**Pretext** will be available in all good bookshops from October 2000.